THE COUNTRY LIVING
Handbook

THE COUNTRY LIVING
Handbook

The best of the good life month by month

DIANA VOWLES

ARCTURUS

ARCTURUS

Arcturus Publishing Limited
26/27 Bickels Yard
151–153 Bermondsey Street
London SE1 3HA

Published in association with
foulsham
W. Foulsham & Co. Ltd,
The Publishing House, Bennetts Close, Cippenham,
Slough, Berkshire SL1 5AP, England

ISBN-13: 978-0-572-03197-8
ISBN-10: 0-572-03197-1

This edition printed in 2006
Copyright © 2006 Arcturus Publishing Limited

All rights reserved

The Copyright Act prohibits (subject to certain very limited exceptions) the making of copies of any copyright work or of a substantial part of such a work, including the making of copies by photocopying or similar process. Written permission to make a copy or copies must therefore normally be obtained from the publisher in advance. It is advisable also to consult the publisher if in any doubt as to the legality of any copying which is to be undertaken.

British Library Cataloguing-in-Publication Data: a catalogue record for this book is available from the British Library

Printed in China

Images reproduced with the permission of the following:
Corbis: 8–9, 11, 12, 13–14, 17, 19, 20–21, 22, 23, 24, 26, 28–29, 31, 32, 33, 34, 36–37, 38, 41, 42, 46, 49, 50, 52–53, 57, 59, 68–69, 71, 72, 75, 76–77, 79, 81, 82–83, 85, 87, 88–89, 92 and all cover images
Sharon Pearson: 6, 44–45, 55, 60–61, 63, 64, 67, 79, 91
Illustrations by Madeleine David: 1, 3, 5, 10, 11, 13 x 2, 16, 18, 23, 25 x 2, 27, 30, 31, 33, 35, 38, 39, 40, 43, 47 x 2, 48 x 2, 51, 54 x 2, 56, 57 x 2, 58, 62, 63, 65, 66, 70 x 2, 71, 73, 74, 78, 79, 80, 84, 85, 86, 90, 91, 93, 94, 95

Contents

Introduction	6
January	8
Discovering woodland	10
Signs of spring	11
The beginnings of a wildlife garden	12
Attracting birds to the garden	12
Nesting sites	13
Decorating a nesting box	13
February	14
Making tracks	16
Pancake Day	17
Making a wildlife pond	18
Pond plants	18
The indoor gardener	19
March	20
Exploring the hedgerows	22
Mad March hares	23
Keeping hens	24
Choosing your hens	24
Rag rugs	26
April	28
Decorating Easter eggs	30
Making a wildflower meadow	32
Making a turf seat	33
Bee-keeping	34
May	36
International dawn chorus day	39
Making a herb garden	40
Drying herbs	41
The merriest month	42
May day	42
Dancing round the maypole	43
The Green Man	43
June	44
The name of a rose	48
Choosing your roses	48
Salads with a difference	50

July	52
Foliage dens	55
Making a potager	56
Exploring the style (of a garden)	56
On the hoof	58
Angora goats	58
Alpacas	58
August	60
Late summer colour	64
Prairie gardens	65
Drying flowers	65
Growing superfoods	66
Blueberries	66
Cranberries	66
Nuts	67
September	68
Growing your own mushrooms	70
Making a hop pillow	71
Wrapping up the summer	72
Sowing afresh	73
Country shows	73
A waddle and a quack	74
Keeping geese	74
Keeping ducks	74

October	76
Sloe gin	78
Making paper for presents	80
Equipment	80
Making the pulp	80
Making the paper	81
November	82
Natural wool dyeing	86
Dye colours and alum mordant	86
December	88
Gilded walnuts	90
Making a pomander	91
Découpage	92
Applying your images	93
Varnishing	93
Making your design	93
Christmas presents	93
Find out more	94
Suppliers	95
Books	95
Index	96

Introduction

IT IS NOT SURPRISING that as the pace of modern life gets ever faster and peace is harder and harder to find in a built-up environment, quieter pastimes and the natural world are growing in their appeal. Thousands of people are leaving the cities to join those who have always preferred green fields and the song of the skylark to choked streets and the roar of the pneumatic drill.

But there's more to living in the country than just inhabiting a rural address. It's essential to understand and enjoy the rhythms of life, to spot the tiny nuances of nature's changes day by day and to take advantage of hobbies and occupations that are hard or even impossible to follow in urban surroundings. While those of us who grew up in the country may do this as naturally as we breathe, newcomers need to adjust to a different pace and a different way of viewing the world: to queue patiently while people exchange news with the village shopkeeper; to accept mud and dog hairs as a part of everyday life; and to realize that the inability to buy that must-have exotic ingredient at 9 p.m. is more than compensated for by the chance to listen to the evening song of a mistle thrush perched atop a dark pine.

This book explores how the seasons change as the year rolls round, and what you can expect to find, both flora and fauna, on your country walks. While sunny summer days hold obvious pleasures, even the coldest and wettest months have something to offer once you go to meet them rather than shutting them out: the architecture of tree skeletons, the evocative, damp aroma of decaying leaves, the sense of a new spring stirring.

You will want to make the most of your garden, too, and if you have sufficient space perhaps embark on keeping some livestock, both as pets and to provide you with food or maybe even wool to dye yourself with colours gathered from the wild. Your garden can also act as a valuable habitat for wildlife, which in its many forms is in retreat from monocultural farmland and its agrichemicals. By planting and cultivating it with an eye to providing food and shelter for birds, hedgehogs and insects you will bring it alive with song and colour that will afford you much enjoyment – and you will make your own very important contribution to country living.

January

With the coming of the New Year, dull days are interspersed with bright cold winter sun, the low angle of its rays backlighting bare stems and silhouetting woodlands and hills. It's too early yet for real signs of spring, but look hard and you will see another year stirring into life.

January

WITH THE CHRISTMAS and New Year's Eve festivities over and the morning's mail of cheerful cards for the mantelpiece replaced by the dull thud of bills, the beginning of January can seem a little flat, especially if you live in town. However, in the country, what is known to gardeners as the dormant season is in fact alive with new growth stirring under the soil, and the hurrying feet of mammals engaged in an urgent quest for food and, soon, a mate and a safe place to rear young. While it may seem tempting to stay in a centrally heated room on a chilly day, taking long walks outdoors can be richly rewarding. Remember the saying: 'There's no such thing as bad weather, only the wrong clothing.'

Discovering Woodland

The best place to observe wildlife now is in woodland, since this provides a warmer and more sheltered environment during the long winter months. At this time of year you can also understand more about the nature of your local broadleaved woods. With the trees laid bare and stark against the sky, it is sometimes easier to identify them by their outline rather than trying to compare leaf shapes when they are in full foliage. Each species has its own characteristic skeleton and these are relatively easy to draw, so you may wish to tuck a notepad and pencils into your pocket with which to make sketches. You can use them for identification purposes later with the help of a reference book.

The woodland habitat generally consists of four layers: a ground layer of small plants such as mosses; a field layer of flowers and ferns; the understorey of hazel, hawthorn, holly, brambles and saplings; and the tree layer, or canopy. The amount of growth you will find in

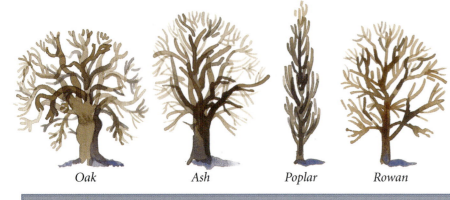

Oak *Ash* *Poplar* *Rowan*

Country vegetable soup

Serves 4–6

After a nippy winter walk there is nothing nicer than to clasp your hands round a bowl of warming homemade soup. If you have bought soup from supermarkets in plastic containers you can reuse these to store portions of soup in the refrigerator, ready to be heated up in minutes.

- 2 tbsp olive oil
- 1 onion, roughly chopped
- 3 celery sticks, finely sliced
- 50g (2oz) mushrooms, finely sliced
- 2 rashers streaky bacon
- 3 carrots, peeled and finely diced
- 3 parsnips, peeled and finely diced
- 2 turnips, peeled and finely diced
- 2 medium leeks, roughly chopped
- 2 tbsp plain flour
- 150ml (1/4 pt) milk
- 900ml (1 1/2 pt) vegetable stock
- 225g (8oz) tomatoes, skinned and roughly chopped
- salt and black pepper
- squeeze of lemon juice
- pinch of thyme and oregano
- parsley to garnish

Heat the oil in a heavy-based pan and fry the onion, celery, mushrooms and bacon over moderate heat until they are softened but not browned. Add the carrots, parsnips, turnips and leeks, fry lightly, then remove the pan from the heat and stir in the flour. Stir in the milk a little at a time.

Return the pan to the heat, add the hot stock and bring to the boil, stirring. Add the tomatoes, stir and bring the soup to a simmer over a low heat. Season to taste with salt, pepper, lemon juice, thyme and oregano, then cover the pan and simmer until the vegetables are well cooked – about 40 minutes. Serve hot, garnished with parsley.

The cold, still, dry days of January make for some spectacular atmospheric scenes

the lower layers depends upon the amount of light that can filter down through the tree layer in full summer. While the loss of large trees in the autumn hurricane of 1987 caused devastation to many well-loved arboreal views, it allowed for spectacular growth in the ground and field layers and gave the wildlife that inhabits them a much-needed boost. In January, you can see the trunks of trees like sentinels stretching into the distance, unmasked from their summer camouflage of surrounding foliage.

Many insects are hiding or hibernating in the leaf mould and in tree bark and you can spot many species of birds hunting them out, including tits, woodpeckers, wrens, robins, nuthatches and blackbirds. You may even hear the latter before you see them as they briskly toss decaying leaves aside in their search for food. You may also see winter migrants from colder northern regions too, such as redwings, waxwings and fieldfares. The winter months are also the most likely time to catch sight of an owl in daylight, since the shortage of food forces them to hunt for many more hours than is necessary in summer.

SIGNS OF SPRING

The ever-popular catkins will already be appearing on hazel bushes, turning from lime green to yellow as the month wears on. Shoots of wild garlic will be sprouting up through the leaf mould, recognizable by their pungent smell if you crush them between your fingers. Now our winters are warmer, you may even find anemones, celandines and primroses in flower.

In the garden, the first spring bulbs will be appearing and the Christmas rose (*Helleborus niger*) will be in flower. Keen gardeners are out there hoeing the flowerbeds and washing out seed trays for this year's propagation; less keen ones restrict themselves to sitting cosily indoors reading seed and bulb catalogues and dreaming of what the garden might be like in summer.

With the arrival of spring, the wildfowl who migrate here from the Arctic regions for the winter will return home to breed, so this is a good time to visit one of the Wildfowl and Wetland Trust sites (see page 95) to see vast flocks of swans, geese and ducks feeding and roosting, before their numbers are depleted. While the January weather doesn't encourage you to remain still and quiet for long in your home woodlands, you may be lucky enough to find space, and knowledgeable companions, in the heated hides of such organizations.

The beginnings of a wildlife garden

WITH THE LOSS OF HABITAT caused by intensive farming, domestic gardens have become crucial to the welfare of many species of bird and mammal. It doesn't require a great deal of effort to make your garden a source of food and shelter for wildlife – and in fact in some regards it takes less effort, because a very tidy garden is not desirable in this context. Decaying seedheads, fallen leaves and pieces of rotten wood will all add to the overall environmental health of the garden. On the active front, providing nesting sites for birds and a wildlife pond (see page 18) are two major ways to begin setting up your garden for a healthy balance of pests and predators that will eliminate the need for chemicals.

Attracting birds to the garden

At this time of year, birds are engaged in a search for food against the clock, with the combination of shorter daylight hours and fewer available insects making survival hard. Putting food out for them is the quickest way to fill your garden with birds which will reward your attentions not only with their song, but also insect control in summer, when it seems the world's supply of aphids must have arrived in your garden.

You can buy a range of feeders designed for seeds or peanuts, and the type you choose will depend upon whether or not you have squirrels in the garden. If you do, a basic wire mesh tube can be emptied in a day, with the mesh bent out of shape. Fortunately, suppliers such as the Royal Society for the Protection of Birds (www.rspb.org.uk) will equip you with more elaborate models where the tube is surrounded by a wire cage that squirrels cannot squeeze through. Be warned that they are capable of taking the feeder away to try at their leisure: if you suspend it from string you may find the string chewed through and the feeder gone. Hanging it from wire instead will prevent that, but if you attach it

By no means dead wood; fallen timber provides shelter and nutrition for myriad plant, fungi and insect species

to a slender branch they are quite capable of chewing through it and making off with the whole lot, leaving you not only without the feeder but with a bit of involuntary pruning too. Suspending the feeder from the type of bracket used for hanging baskets, attached to a tree trunk or shed, will thwart them.

Also available is a squirrel guard in the form of a plastic dome to place over the top of hanging feeders. With a pole feeder, the dome can simply be inverted to provide a baffle to prevent squirrels climbing the pole.

Provide a range of food suitable for different species. Coconuts, peanuts, seeds, oatmeal, maize and jacket potatoes will keep most garden birds happy. Thrushes and blackbirds love apple cores and grapes: you may find your local greengrocer is happy to sell you overripe ones cheaply. Soak dried fruit and bread before putting them out to prevent them swelling in birds' stomachs, and always buy peanuts and seeds from reputable sources to avoid dangerous toxins. You can also buy suet cakes with nuts and seeds in them, but these are very easy to make by simply melting some suet in a bowl and stirring in whatever you wish to add. Mealworms, available from suppliers such as the RSPB, are a natural food that will crawl away from the feeder if they can, so put them in a container with slippery sides. Do not offer maggots: they are commercially produced carrion eaters and may contain various contaminants.

Place feeders about 2–3m (6$\frac{1}{2}$–10ft) from a bush or tree, so that the birds feel they have a place of hiding to flee to if necessary. Clean them, and the ground underneath, from time to time to prevent the buildup of disease-causing bacteria.

Birds also need water, both for drinking and for bathing. A whole range of birdbaths is available commercially, or you may prefer to use a simple wide dish with sloping sides. A bathing bird is particularly vulnerable to cats, so site the bath clear of foliage but within a few metres of cover for the bird to flee to.

Nesting sites

Rotting trees provide excellent nesting sites for many birds, but there are fewer and fewer of them to be found as our landscape becomes increasingly managed. Consequently, your contribution is very valuable. Nest boxes of various types, suitable for birds ranging from blue tits to owls, are easily available. The autumn is the best time to put them up, but now is not too late: birds are just beginning to look for nests in January.

Where they are sited is important, or they may remain uninhabited. Nest boxes for robins have more open fronts than those designed for tits, so to avoid

predation they need to be well hidden in foliage. Position tit boxes about 2m (6$\frac{1}{2}$ft) up a wall or tree trunk, not one that has branches nearby for a cat to crouch on. Don't place the nestbox so that it faces south, as the eggs and chicks will become too hot in the sunshine; and don't place it near a feed table as the comings and goings of feeding birds will disturb the inhabitants.

Decorating a nest box

It is not hard to make your own nest boxes, but making a basic box is not a particularly fulfilling task when they can be bought for £10 or so. If you would like to be creative in this department, it is more satisfying to buy a plain nest box made of plywood or MDF and decorate it, perhaps in colours to suit your house if it is on your wall, or with a design of flowers and leaves against a tree trunk.

If you prefer a very rustic look, split small branches lengthwise, trim them to length and glue them to the nest box, taking care not to alter the dimensions of the hole in a tit box.

February

This is the month when you may wake up to find a grey and gloomy day or a scene of stunning beauty with sunshine lighting up the hoar frost on your garden. But underneath even the hardest frost, spring is beginning to stir.

February

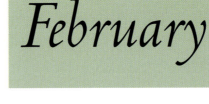

FEBRUARY IS often thought of as a gloomy month, but these days it's the time when we are most likely to see snow, an increasingly unusual sight in southern lowland areas, and one that brings huge excitement for children and a good deal to enjoy for adults, too. Familiar landscapes take on a whole new form and wrapping up warm to enjoy a brisk walk, feet crunching through the snow, is a particular pleasure of the season.

Yet this is also the month when the snowdrops and celandines make their appearance in the woodlands and verges and buds begin to fatten on the tree branches. In your garden, spring bulbs will be sprouting through the soil and the lovely smell of damp earth and new greenery enliven the spirits and promise spring.

By now frogs and toads are rousing from their winter hibernation, and if the season is mild you may see early frog- and toadspawn in ponds. Contrary to general belief, badgers don't hibernate and February is a good time to watch out for them at dusk and dawn. Although you won't see them until later in the spring, the cubs are born now and there will be much activity to alert you to the presence of a sett. You may notice fresh heaps of soil where tunnels have been dug, or piles of dead vegetation outside, that point to a bit of housekeeping below ground. Sitting quietly and patiently downwind of the sett (remember not to wear clothing that rustles) gives you the best chance of seeing the adult inhabitants.

Birds are beginning to pair up, and the volume of song increases

MAKING TRACKS

In February snow or indeed February mud, you can have fun identifying tracks to discover the wildlife and domestic animals that have been out and about.

1 Ground birds have three toes pointing forwards and a short toe pointing backwards. This group includes game birds, waterfowl (ducks, geese and swans) and waders such as gulls and avocets. A walking bird leaves an alternating pattern of feet and you will be able to guess at the size of the bird by the length of its gait.

2 Perching birds form a large group ranging from blue tits to eagles. The footprint here is of three toes pointing forwards and a longer one pointing backwards. You will recognize birds that hop by the neat pairs of tracks side by side.

3 Squirrels have a splay-footed outline with four pads and five toes.

4 Dogs have four toes and toe pads with a larger pad behind them.

5 A badger has an unmistakeable triangular footprint with five long toes and distinctive pads.

6 Sheep and deer are two-toed, with deer easily distinguishable by their longer stride.

The bright green tips of emerging bulbs are often one of the first signs of spring

Pancake Day

The custom of eating pancakes on Shrove Tuesday dates back many centuries and derives from the preparation for the Lenten fast. The three days before Lent, known as Shrovetide, were the last chance to enjoy tasty food – and empty the larder – before the fast until Easter. Pancakes traditionally were made with the remaining eggs.

It's not known exactly when the custom of pancake races began, but the pancake race at Olney in Buckinghamshire has been held ever since 1445. According to the rules, any female resident over the age of sixteen wearing an apron and a covering on her head can take part, carrying a frying pan with a pancake that must be tossed three times during the race. Pancake races became popular after the Second World War, perhaps just from the novelty of having eggs to waste once rationing was over.

throughout the month as they strive to attract mates and defend their territory. You can give them a hand with nest building by putting out hair from your hairbrush, dried grass, wool and pet hair. A hanging basket with dead vegetation and moss left over from the previous year is a rich source of nest-building material for many species (before you pull it apart, make sure that it has not already become this year's nest site for a wren or robin).

Pancakes
Makes 8–10 pancakes

- 100g (4oz) plain flour
- pinch of salt
- 2 eggs, lightly beaten
- 300ml (½ pint) milk
- butter for frying
- 50g (2oz) caster sugar
- 2 lemons

Sift the flour and salt into a large bowl then, using a wooden spoon, make a hollow in the centre and pour the eggs into it. Gradually pour half the milk into the flour, working it in as you go.

Beat the mixture with the spoon or a whisk until it is free of lumps. Leave to stand for a few minutes then add the remaining milk, beating continuously. The batter should have the same consistency as single cream.

Heat an 18cm (7in) frying pan and melt just enough butter in it to grease the pan. When the butter is hot, pour in enough batter to form a thin layer (about 2 tbsp) and tip the pan to spread it all over the base. It should take less than a minute for the bottom of the pancake to become golden (lift the edge with a palette knife to check). Then flip the pancake over with the palette knife or practise your pancake-tossing skills by holding the pan away from you and giving it a quick flick.

Slide the pancake out of the pan on to a warm plate, sprinkle it with sugar and squeeze some lemon juice over it. Fold it in half twice, cover with foil and place over a pan of simmering water to keep warm while you make the remaining pancakes one by one.

Making a wildlife pond

A NATURAL-LOOKING POND, surrounded by vegetation, will offer a valuable habitat to many species of wildlife and will bring you benefits too, such as the presence of frogs (which will dine on your slugs), dragonflies, mayflies and even herons and ducks. If you are short of space, even an old sink or upturned dustbin lid will do, but if you are able to allocate more space you will find that it pays dividends by making your garden a more attractive and interesting place to be in.

Choose a site that will be in shade for part of the day, but avoid overhanging trees or you will spend autumn fishing out dead leaves. If your garden slopes, the pond will look more natural at the bottom of the slope. Mark out the shape with a hosepipe or string; an irregular shape will look most natural. Dig out the pond, varying the depth and making sure to provide sloping edges in case creatures such as hedgehogs fall in. Areas about 5–20cm (2–8in) deep will allow you to put in marginal plants, adding to the natural look. Aim for a depth of at least 90cm (3ft) elsewhere so that pond-dwellers will be able to find protection from both heat and cold.

Remove any stones that might puncture the pond liner and put down sand, old carpet or underlay to protect it. Line the pond with flexible butyl liner, which is easily obtainable from garden centres. Ideally, fill your pond from water butts, but if your pond is a large one, you will need to resort to tap water. This is likely to encourage algae which will turn the water green, but this will clear as a natural balance is established. A couple of buckets of water from a neighbour's pond will introduce the organisms needed to give your pond a kick start.

Allow the pond to settle for a couple of weeks, and then you can start on the fun stuff – planting. You will need a variety of oxygenating, floating, deep water and marginal plants. Native species are best, and some foreign species should be avoided at all cost as they spread uncontrollably in British waterways (see box). Plants in the immediate vicinity of the pond could be any garden plant, but clearly some will suit the natural look better than others. Long ornamental grasses will lead convincingly to the pond, for example, while a bed of hybrid tea roses would spoil the effect entirely. Once you have planted, importing some frogspawn will bring you frogs in short order; collect it in a plastic bag (preferably from a neighbour's pond) and tip it gently into your own pond. Collecting frogspawn from the wild is not illegal, but is deemed 'inappropriate' by some countryside groups. However, considering the falling numbers of frogs, as a result of fewer ponds and the infill of ditches, starting up your own frog colony could be seen as redressing the balance. Don't forget that fish will often eat frogspawn and newly hatched frogs, so if you want a fish pond, the two will probably not cohabit happily.

Pond Plants

Oxygenating plants
- *Aponogeton distachyos* (Water hawthorn)
- *Ceratophyllum demersum* (Hornwort)
- *Hottonia palustris* (water violet)
- *Myriophyllum spicatum* (Spiked water milfoil)
- *Potamogeton crispus* (Curly pondweed)

Floating plants
- *Hydrocharis morsus-ranae* (Frogbit)

Deep-water plants
- *Nuphar luteum* (Yellow water lily)
- *Nymphaea alba* (White water lily)
- *Orontium aquaticum* (Golden club)
- *Ranunculus aquatilis* (Water crowfoot)

Marginals
- *Acorus calamus* (Sweet-scented rush)
- *Butomus umbellatus* (Flowering rush)
- *Calla palustris* (Bog arum)
- *Caltha palustris* (Marsh marigold)
- *Iris pseudacorus* (Yellow flag)
- *Myosotis scorpioides* (Water forget-me-not)

Some plants to avoid
- *Azolla filiculoides* (Water fern)
- *Crassula helmsii* (Australian swamp stonecrop)
- *Eichhornia crassipes* (Water hyacinth)
- *Elodea canadensis* (Canadian pondweed)
- *Hydrocotyle ranunculoides* (Floating pennywort)

The indoor gardener

AT THIS TIME OF YEAR the weather often discourages active gardening and it can be hard to spur yourself on, even if you try to visualize yourself sitting outside on balmy summer days surrounded by glorious flowers.

Cleaning out last year's flowerpots can be done in a greenhouse or utility room, and painting some in cheerful designs will help you look forward to adorning your garden with pretty container plants. All you need is some acrylic paints, a broad paintbrush and your artistic imagination.

First, make sure the outside of the pot is clean. Lay one colour all over the pot, then paint your designs on top of that. It is best to confine yourself to a maximum of four colours or the end result may look too jumbled. A white background with vertical stripes in three colours and varying widths will give a jaunty seaside look, or you may wish to limit yourself to just two colours for a more restrained effect. Keep in mind your favourite container plants while you work so that your choice of paint colours will complement them.

Buying plants from your local garden centre is often more expensive than ordering them from mail order specialist nurseries and seed catalogues, and certainly the choice isn't as wide. Making planting plans now and settling yourself into a comfortable chair with a pile of catalogues will give you a head start. If plants have already arrived by mail order, for example roses, and the weather is too bad to plant them out, pack damp compost round them and put them in a sheltered place, watering them if necessary.

Once established, a wildlife pond is a wonderful focal point in a garden

March

Lengthening days, brightening skies and a light green haze of buds on the trees tell us that spring is on the way. Everywhere there is the sense of new growth and new life burgeoning as the woods and hedgerows come alive with spring flowers and nesting birds. In the garden, too, favourite flowers are beginning to make their annual contribution to the scene.

March

CLIMATE CHANGE means that nowadays March very often comes in like a lamb rather than a lion, but even if the season is a wet, cold and windy one the days are lengthening. And along with this comes birdsong, fattening buds on the trees and all the other signs of spring that we love.

The daffodils in the Lake District that inspired Wordsworth to write his famous verses of poetry long ago were no doubt the wild variety (*Narcissus pseudonarcissus*), growing as they were beside the lake, beneath the trees. Whether you are lucky enough to come across the delicate wild species or you have planted more brash hybrids in your garden, the sight of their yellow flowers blowing in the breeze speaks perhaps more potently of an English spring than anything else. Lambs, those other heart-lifting symbols of spring, are gambolling in the fields, and the first butterflies of the year are beginning to appear.

So too are an advance party of migrating birds from Africa, including sand martins, the champion weightlifters of the bird world: after a round trip of 8,000km (5,000 miles) or more they set to work building a nest site, excavating sand to a volume forty times their body weight of 13g ($^1/_2$oz). In human terms, that is equivalent to a person of 76kg (12 stone) shifting 3 tonnes – without any tools.

EXPLORING THE HEDGEROWS

During the Second World War, Britain found its reliance on food imports a dangerous thing, scraping by with severe food rationing and a hasty despatch of 'land girls' to work on the farms. After the war ended the emphasis was on the self-sufficiency of food, and that meant putting every scrap of land into production. Hedges took up space and halted machinery in its tracks, so they were grubbed up in their thousands; nearly 402,500km (250,000 miles) of hedgerow have been lost since 1945. However, preservation orders have been put on some ancient hedges, and farmers have planted up to 6,000 miles of hedge in the last ten years thanks to charities such as LEAF (Linking Environment And Farming). LEAF helps farmers to implement better environmental practice on farms, including hosting visits to demonstrate to the public and other farmers that it is possible to link the environment with farming. Visit their website (www.leafuk.org) to find out more about them.

Hedges not only provide shelter, food and breeding sites for many birds, mammals and insects, they also provide corridors across the landscape along which wildlife can travel in safety. Up to ten pairs of birds can breed in 1km ($^1/_2$ mile) of hedge, with a food source close to hand. Later in the year, hedgerow plants will provide seed to see them through the winter. In March, the hedges are decked with blackthorn blossom, followed by hawthorn, wild honeysuckle, dog roses and guelder rose. At their foot, you can usually find flowers of the woodland edge such as bluebells and primroses. Walking quietly alongside a hedge as dusk falls, listening to the rustling of small mammals and the final notes of birdsong, and smelling the fresh scent of new-growing plants, gives a sense like nothing else can of the earth preparing for another season.

Most hedges were planted in the eighteenth and nineteenth

Hares are in decline, for the most part due to a change in farming practices

A typical English countryside lane, with overhanging trees just coming into bud

MAD MARCH HARES

The wild antics of leaping and boxing hares that gave rise to the expression 'mad as a March hare' are in fact just part of their mating rituals. This behaviour is not, in fact, confined to March, as their breeding season lasts from January to October. However, you are more likely to see it in early spring before the crops and hay meadows grow tall enough to hide them.

Hares are much bigger than rabbits, reaching 48–70cm (19–28in) in length, with black-tipped ears much longer in relation to the size of their head. Their legs, too, are longer, enabling them to reach a speed of 56kmh (35mph). You won't find signs of their presence by looking for rabbit-like burrows as they bring up their young (leverets) in shallow hollows in the ground.

The most likely place to see hares is in lowland areas with traditional mixed farming methods, though they are also seen on golf courses and sand dunes. Early morning and evening are the best time to go looking for them, as this is when they are most active. Two hares boxing will probably be males fighting over a female, or perhaps a female discouraging an amorous male. These beautiful creatures are in decline, largely as a result of changed farming methods, but the UK Biodiversity Action Plan (www.ukbap.org.uk) aims to double numbers to about two million by the year 2010. To see if you can play a part in helping the hare, contact your local Wildlife Trust (www.wildlifetrusts.org).

centuries, when a succession of laws contained in the Enclosure Acts between 1760 and 1830 replaced the open land system of farming with fields bounded by fences or hedges. Again, the necessity to produce more food was the cause. Previously farmers had tended to own many scattered strips of land, which was inefficient in terms of using new machinery and practising crop rotation schemes. The new laws redistributed plots of land and required farmers to enclose them with boundaries, and so the patchwork of fields that still typifies large parts of the British landscape came into being. There are, though, some hedges dating back to the medieval era, the remnants of ancient woodland.

You can estimate the date of a hedge by counting the number of woody plant species, including trees, you find in a 30m (33yd) length of it. Multiply the number of species by 100: if there are three species, for example, the hedge is likely to be about 300 years old.

Ash

Horse chestnut

Sycamore

Keeping hens

THE PRACTICE OF KEEPING a few hens, both as pets and as a source of delicious fresh eggs, is increasing in popularity, even in towns. The urban poultry keeper with a taste for cutting-edge design can buy a neat kit of a plastic hutch and fox-proof run with, in some areas, two chickens, and a driver to set up the equipment and give a crash course on handling the birds (see page 95). In the country, with a spacious garden, it's possible to enjoy keeping a whole flock with the benefit of a steady supply of eggs and plentiful manure for the garden, too.

Choosing your hens

Some varieties of hen have famous names, such as Buff Orpingtons and Rhode Island Reds, but unless you wish to go in for serious egg production you can choose from any number of splendidly feathered types of bird. Cochin chickens, originally imported from the Far East in the nineteenth century, are the giants of the chicken world, with blowsily feathered legs and feet and a range of colours including blue (actually a beautiful greyish mauve). Popular with hobbyists for the show ring, they will produce sufficient eggs for a family. Brahmas, stately birds with striking colouring, are their close relatives, while for a really notable look Silkies can't be beaten, with feathers lacking barbs or quills and giving an appearance not unlike a Persian cat.

If you like brown eggs, Marans are the birds for you, producing eggs so dark as to be chocolate-coloured; Welsummers will give you a good supply of terracotta-coloured eggs; Buff Orpingtons and Light Sussex produce light cream eggs, while Cream Legbars lay blue eggs.

If you are not choosy about the appearance of the chickens and their eggs, taking in hens rescued from battery cages will give you the satisfaction of giving a bird a longer and better life. In battery farms, the lighting is controlled to encourage a higher production of eggs than would normally be the case, with the result that by the time a year is up the hens are considered 'spent' and sent for slaughter. Given a new home as pets, with perhaps some eggs as a bonus, the hens will live another two or three years.

A battery hen is kept in a cage smaller than a piece of A4 paper and has no perch to roost on, so when they first arrive at your home you can expect them to have few feathers and be totally unaccustomed to freedom and daylight. Their legs will not be strong, so provide a ramp for them to reach their roost. They will usually have been debeaked, giving them a shovel-shaped bottom beak, but foraging free-range will restore the natural shape. At first they will probably sleep on the floor of their roost, but as they adapt to natural conditions instinct will often guide

The bright, warm colours of the Buff Orpington are a familiar sight on farms

Zabaglione

Serves 4

This classic Italian dessert, said to have been invented for the sixteenth-century Medici court in Florence, is traditionally served warm, though if you prefer you can also try it cold. Recipes vary as to the proportions and nature of the ingredients, but the end result is always a sinfully rich and sweet dessert. You can substitute Madeira or sweet sherry for the Marsala.

- 4 egg yolks
- 50g (2oz) caster sugar
- 90ml (3fl oz) Madeira
- sponge fingers to serve

Place the eggs, sugar and Madeira in a mixing bowl and whisk them together until the mixture is pale and creamy.

Set the bowl over a pan of barely simmering water and whisk the mixture continuously until it is thick and fluffy. This should take 7–10 minutes but if it requires longer do not raise the heat or the mixture may curdle. Pour into warmed wine glasses and serve immediately.

them to the perch. If not, you can lift them gently on to it at dusk to give them the idea.

Feeding

You will need to give your hens a pelleted proprietary feed, preferably organic, but if not, one suitable for free-range hens. The feed will contain the necessary nutrients, vitamins and minerals, but scattering grain on the ground will give the hens a reason to follow their instinct to scratch about and will also encourage them to range more widely. Although free-range hens will pick up stones if they are available, you should also provide poultry grit which helps to break down the grain in the bird's gizzard. Unless it is included in the proprietary feed, give crushed oyster shell, which contains calcium and thus makes for strong eggshells.

The hens will also enjoy kitchen scraps, but do not give them any with meat or salt in them. The yellowness of eggs' yolks depends on the amount of chlorophyll the hens eat (battery eggs are artificially coloured), so give them vegetables such as cabbage, or turnip and beetroot tops. If the hens are in a run, tying the vegetables in a bundle and hanging it up for them to peck at will keep them happily occupied. Battery hens will have been fed on layers' mash, so be sure to offer that for the first few weeks to aid them in their transition to a different diet.

Fresh, clean water should always be available, placed in the shade in warm weather as hens don't like to drink warm water. And, of course, apart from breeds such as Marans, which roost in trees, hens should be shut safely away from foxes at dusk.

Once you have mastered the basic rules of keeping hens, you will find them very little trouble to look after; and during summer days in the garden you will gain the extra reward of relaxing to the sound of contemplative clucking from happy hens.

Rag Rugs

THERE IS HUGE satisfaction to be gained from making a rag rug, combining as it does the chance to be creative, the recycling of old materials and the continuation of an old and appealing tradition and craft. In the nineteenth century, rag rugs were much favoured by Shaker and Amish communities: with their ethos of pursuing a simple life where nothing was wasted, a rag rug was a wonderful way of keeping busy, but in a leisurely way. These sorts of rugs were also popular among farming families in England and Scandinavia.

Because rag rugs, however attractively designed, were generally given hard wear, few remain from the nineteenth century. While in some households they were laid upside down, to be turned upright, clean and bright, when visitors arrived, they were moved from room to room as they became more and more worn; a splendid new rug laid with some ceremony in the parlour would eventually be relegated to a bedroom or the kitchen and maybe even the dog's bed before ending its life on the compost heap.

The methods of making a rag rug varied. The early settlers in America just plaited old cloth and coiled it round, rather like a giant seagrass table mat, while in Scandinavia, where there is a strong tradition of handweaving, they were made on looms. Most commonly, though, jute feed sacks were used as a backing through which strips of fabric were hooked or prodded.

Inspiration for your designs can come from anywhere; a seasonal theme is always lovely and will serve to remind you when you made your rug

Some rugs were strictly utilitarian – just a means of keeping the occupants' feet off the cold floor throughout the winter – but usually, after the feed sack was unpicked and washed, a design was drawn on it. Depending on the creative skill of the rugmaker, this might be flowers, fruit, animals and the prettier insect species such as butterflies or ladybirds, or biblical stories; or, for the artistically unconfident, a simple message such as 'welcome home'. The rags were then torn up, into short strips for prodded rugs or longer strips for hooked rugs, sewn end-to-end if need be.

Rag rugs began to fall from favour in the 1920s and became a rare sight with the advent of fitted carpets after the Second World War. Today they are popular once more for the homespun appearance that is redolent of country life.

MAKING A RAG RUG

Rag rugs are best made from cotton or wool fabrics, as synthetics will attract the dirt more. Cotton rugs, in either cool or jazzy colours, will look great in summer while a woollen rug with plenty of hot reds in it will be a warming sight by the winter hearth. You will no doubt have fabric to hand such as old bed linen, dresses, jerseys, tweed and so forth, and friends will probably be amused to contribute unwanted clothes that will reappear in a new guise on your floor. Failing all else, remnant sales and car boot sales will provide plenty of scope. Wash all your fabrics to make sure they do not shrink unevenly when you wash your rug at a later date.

You will need loosely woven fabric for the backing. If you want to follow the ethos of recycling, you may be able to obtain meal sacks from grocery or wholefood shops; an easier option is to buy some hessian. The only equipment you require is a rug hook or large crochet hook and, to make handling the rug easier, a rectangular quilting frame to which you attach the hessian. For your first attempt, it's best to go for a very easy design

Take inspiration from nature: a small tortoiseshell butterfly

such as stripes and a small size of mat so that you don't become too discouraged.

Once you have cleaned and hemmed your backing, draw a design on the fabric with a wax crayon. The rug is worked right side up, from side to side and top to bottom if you are using a frame, or from the centre outwards if there is no frame to keep an even tension.

Hold a strip of fabric beneath the hessian with your left hand (if you are right-handed), with one end at the point where you wish to start. Then push the hook down through the hessian and pull the end of the strip up through the fabric. Make the next hole as near to the first as you can, and bring up enough of the fabric strip to make a loop about 1cm ($^1/_2$in) high. Repeat until you reach the end of the strip, pulling the end up to the surface and trimming it to the same length as the loops. Start your next strip in the same hole as this end strip.

Clean your rug by hanging it over the washing line and beating the dust out of it. If need be, you can wash it with carpet shampoo and hang it out in the sunshine to dry.

April

The fresh breezes of April still carry a nip on some days, but on others they are warm and balmy, promising the arrival of longer days and outdoor delights such as lunch outside with salad and a glass of wine. The hedgerows are starting to bloom with wildflowers, and native birds are hatching their first broods.

April

THIS IS THE MONTH when some of our best-loved migrant birds such as swallows and housemartins begin to wing in, just as vast flocks of waterfowl and waders are on their passage back to their summer breeding sites in the Arctic regions. In the gardens, hedgerows and woodlands, fresh flowers are opening almost daily; yellow cowslips bloom on grassy banks, and in shady woodland spots yellow archangel is pushing its way up through the leaf mould and brushwood. On warm days, dandelion clocks are already dispersing in puffs of silver on the spring breezes.

One of the greatest spring panoramas is unfolding now – swards of brilliant bluebells carpeting the woodland floor. So popular is this sight that people will travel miles to see the most famous bluebell woods, such as Bradfield Woods near Bury St Edmunds or Maplehurst Wood near Hastings.

Today our bluebells are under threat from the illegal digging up of wild bulbs for sale at nurseries – and that means digging up by organized groups with heavy machinery, not the occasional person with a spade – and by hybridization with the Spanish bluebell (*Hyacinthoides hispanica*), a bigger, scentless variety. Planting native bluebells (*Hyacinthoides non-scriptus*) rather than foreign species in your garden is a way of helping our native species to survive.

The creamy blossom of wild cherry, or gean (*Prunus avium*), is another lovely April sight, bedecking woodland edges with a snowy border even as the days grow warmer. In fruit orchards, you may spot bullfinches feeding on flower buds, easily distinguishable from other finches by their rosy-pink breasts. With their numbers halved in the last twenty-five years from loss of habitat in mature mixed woodlands, these finches are a sight to cherish.

Decorating Easter Eggs

In the days when Lent was strictly observed by many people, eggs could not be eaten, so they were preserved or hard-boiled to keep them until Easter – hence the popularity of Easter eggs.

Your choices for decorating Easter eggs are many and varied, but first you need to blow the eggs. Using a needle, make a hole at one end of the shell and a slightly larger one at the other end, working the needle round to make sure you have pierced the membrane round the yolk. Holding the egg over a bowl, blow through the smaller hole until the contents of the shell are forced out the other end.

As ever, decorating is a matter of taste and if you feel you want to stick rhinestones all over your eggs there's nothing to stop you! But often the simplest things are the most attractive and keep in tune with the seasons, too. Dyeing them with natural colours gives subtle shades and allows you to exercise your imagination with what is available in the kitchen and garden. Put the eggs in a single layer in a pan, cover with water and a teaspoon of vinegar and add any of the following:

Onion skin	*golden colour*
Gorse flowers	*light yellow*
Spinach	*green*
Coffee	*dark brown*
Cochineal	*red*
Turmeric	*deep yellow*
Beetroot	*red*
Blueberries/red cabbage	*blue*

Bring the water to a boil then simmer for 15 minutes. Remove the eggs to a bowl, or, if you want a darker shade, leave them in the dye overnight.

By now, swans have built their reed nests on the rivers and skylarks are singing above the fields. The first tadpoles are beginning to emerge in ponds and the call of the cuckoo puts the winter firmly in the past; horse chestnut trees are adorned with their flowering candles and the glorious song of the wren cannot fail to lift the heart. Equally cheering is the sight of ducklings taking their first dives and fizzing back up to the surface of the water like fluffy brown champagne corks. If you are lucky, you may be able to watch young mammals such as badger cubs at play, or maybe even catch a quick sighting of a migratory osprey heading for Scotland or the Lake District to breed.

At Easter, the first bank holiday of the year, town-dwellers head for the countryside in their thousands to rediscover their roots in nature. It seems that no matter how urban their everyday lives, the British still cherish the concept of themselves as essentially country-dwellers with mud on their boots and dogs asleep by the range, its oven churning out batches of hot cakes or a hearty casserole.

Getting down to rivers and streams to spot ducklings is one of April's delights

Making a wildflower meadow

MOST OF THE WILDFLOWER meadows that once covered vast tracts of British countryside are long gone beneath the impact of herbicides that wipe out everything except the desired crop, taking with them numerous insects, birds and mammals that depended on them for food and breeding habitats. However, if you are able to spend even a few minutes in a wildflower meadow, either one managed by a regional Wildlife Trust or one that has simply survived through the absence of intensive farming, you will be astonished at the sights, scents and sounds everyone took for granted before the mid-twentieth century: flowers clustered so thickly that the eye can see a haze of colour far into the distance; sweet fragrances carried on the air; and the steady drone of bees and other insects gathering nectar and distributing pollen.

Fortunately, conservationists are now planning to re-create wildflower meadows in various sites and you can do your bit for the environment – and give yourself some low-maintenance gardening – by setting aside part of your garden as a wildflower meadow, however small.

The type and profusion of flowers in the wild obviously depends upon the climate and soil type, and you will need to establish which flowers would naturally grow in your area. Choose the wrong wild flowers and you will simply be wasting your money, as they will not survive; the essence of this type of gardening is to let nature take its course, rather than trying to lime or acidify small areas of soil to suit a particular garden plant you have set your heart on. Suppliers of wildflower seeds sometimes sell particular mixes of plants designed for a soil type, or they will give you advice on which plug plants to buy.

Turf seats may take time to really establish themselves, but the resulting effects can be beautiful

Seeds or plug plants?

The choice between seeds and plug plants depends on your budget and how much work you want to do. Wildflower seeds cannot battle against thick grass and they also prefer soil with low fertility, so if you are planning to convert some of your lawn, you will need to remove squares of turf and topsoil to provide areas to sow seed that has a chance of germinating. Be warned that if you sow in spring, you may not see any flowers until the following summer, as many wildflower seeds need a period of winter cold to germinate. In such a site, unless it is a very large one, plug plants are probably the better option for a faster and easier result, though the range of species available will not be as wide.

If you are starting on bare soil, sowing wildflower seed is much easier. Just strip off the top 5–10cm (2–4in) of soil to reduce fertility then rake and roll the soil to make a seed bed. Seed lightly with a natural grass mix such as bent and fescue grasses (about 1–1.5g seed per square metre), then sow the wildflower seeds. These will probably be very small, so mix them with sand to make even distribution easier. Rake the soil lightly and firm with a roller.

Cut your newly sown meadow when the grass reaches about 10cm (4in) high to deter weeds (such as chickweed), and for the first year follow by cutting the meadow every six to eight weeks, removing the cuttings to prevent the build-up of dead thatch. Thereafter, cut the meadow once in late March or early April to deter vigorous grasses and thistles and then again in late August, when the flowers and grass species will have had a chance to set seed. This can be done with a hand scythe or a strimmer. Even better, if you have goats (see page 58) they will do the job for you, and provide useful fertilizer into the bargain!

Making a turf seat

In medieval times, two of the most popular garden types were the 'herber' and the 'flowery mead'. The former fulfilled a practical purpose, providing plants for cookery and for medicine, and also acted as a place of retreat and relaxation. The latter was purely aesthetic and consisted of a meadow studded with flowers such as daisies, primroses, columbines and forget-me-nots. Also common in the medieval garden were turf seats, where one could sit and contemplate the wonders of nature.

Turf seats are becoming increasingly fashionable today, lending their ancient charm and according with the current desire to create with the environment rather than to impose upon it. Should you wish to add fragrance too, you can use the same principle but plant with creeping thyme or chamomile instead.

If you have a sloping bank in your garden, you can dig out your seat rather than building it up. Dig out the backrest first, to a width of about 1.5m (5ft) and depth of 45cm (18in) or so, and clear away the grass at the top to a width of about 5cm (2in). Next, dig out a flat seat at right angles to the base of your backrest and rake the soil smooth.

Begin placing the new turf, starting with the lip and butting it up to the edge of the grass. If any of it starts to slip down, anchor it by pushing wire through the turf into the earth beneath (a bent wire coat hanger will do the job splendidly).

On flat ground you will have to build upwards instead, using a wooden or metal framework. Railway sleepers are easy to obtain and handle, but don't use second-hand ones reclaimed from railways as they will be impregnated with tar and creosote – you should be able to find new ones in a good garden centre. Pack the framework with at least 5cm (2in) of soil on which to lay the turf.

Bee-keeping

FOR A REALLY SOOTHING experience, there's little to beat relaxing in a hammock beneath the trees, a cooling drink to hand and the steady hum of honey bees working their way from flower to flower providing the background music. Plant a nectar-rich garden and the bees will find you – but why not set up a hive of your own so that you will benefit from their honey, too?

You don't need much space to be a bee-keeper. Perhaps surprisingly, keeping hives is becoming increasingly popular with town-dwellers and there are thought to be about 5,000 beehives in London, the last place one associates with rural joys. Not only that, the honey can be of high quality because of the huge range of plants within the bees' range compared to what they find on intensively farmed land. If their garden is too small, some urban bee-keepers have hives on a flat roof or on an allotment.

Honey bees live in colonies that can have as many as 50,000 members, and as the colony grows the bees will solve overcrowding by swarming in late spring; about half the hive leave and collect somewhere nearby until a new home is decided upon. This may be in the garden of your neighbour, who will understandably regard you as responsible for dealing with what may seem a rather alarming intrusion. Consequently, you need to take the management of your hives seriously and to learn the ropes. Contacting the British Beekeepers' Association (see page 94) is the best way to start: the association exists to promote beekeeping and is keen to encourage new people. It will put you in touch with experienced beekeepers to help you through the early stages, advise you on buying equipment and link you up with a local association where you can meet other members. It also runs courses and provides online support boards.

You will need to make some outlay at the start: a new hive will set you back about £250 (it's best to avoid second-hand hives since they may carry disease), and you will need full protective clothing and a smoker. You can buy bees guaranteed to be disease-free, though in late spring you may have the chance to obtain a swarm from a local beekeeper.

A worker bee will visit up to 1,000 flowers on a single trip, carrying about 40mcg (0.04g) of nectar back

Honey on tap – keeping a hive will also help promote Britain's bee population

to the hive, half of which may evaporate before it is stored as honey. Producing 450g (1lb) of honey may require more than 200,000 foraging trips, and a typical colony's range may cover 104m^2 (40 square miles). Before she reaches her status as a forager, at the age of twenty days, the bee will have spent her first twelve days cleaning cells, nursing the brood and tending the queen and her next eight days building the comb and storing nectar and pollen brought by forager bees. On becoming a forager, she has about ten busy days or so of collecting nectar before she dies.

Meanwhile, the sole purpose of the male bees, or drones, is to mate with the queen; they do no work in the hives at all. But when food supplies are low and the weather is cold, the worker bees boot them out of the hives to perish, and those that do mate with the queen die in the process.

But perhaps the most interesting aspect of bees is their communication system, most famously the waggle dance which lets the watching 'recruit' bees know where a forager has found a good source of nectar. She performs this dance as soon as she returns to the hive, on an area near the entrance. Dancing in a figure of eight pattern, she indicates the direction of the source by the angle she follows in relation to the sun, and the distance from the hive by the length of time she waggles her abdomen: each extra 75 milliseconds adds roughly 100m (330ft) in distance. The explanation of the waggle dance as being a kind of map-drawing process was first posited in the 1960s, but was proved only recently by the use of radio transponders after suggestions that the bees in fact followed scent. Capturing recruit bees as they left the hives and releasing them 250m (820ft) away, scientists observed that they travelled a path not to the feeding site but one that exactly followed the flight that had been outlined for them by the dancer.

The honey you will gain from your bees will have antibacterial and antimicrobial properties that are sometimes lost in commercial production, and eating local honey is thought to help hay-fever sufferers. You can expect a yield of about 13–22kg (30–50lb) from one hive each season: plenty to distribute to the neighbours so that they will appreciate the presence of your bees. If you decide to sell it, you will not need a licence but you should contact your local Trading Standards Office to check the details of what you will need to put on the label.

BUMBLE BEES

Bumble bees won't produce honey but they will pollinate your plants and, as they are declining – one of the 15 British sub-species was declared extinct in 1999 – there's a good case for encouraging them in your garden. They are easily distinguishable from honey bees by their much greater size and louder buzz. It's thought that part of the reason for their dwindling numbers is that most of the species have long tongues and like tubular flowers such as vetches, thistles and knapweed – the type of flowers found in traditional hay meadows – which are increasingly rare. There are plans to supply conservation seed mixes with nectar-rich tubular flowers to farmers, and you can do your bit to preserve our native species by planting such species in your garden.

Bumble bees nest in burrows, and you can provide a habitat for them by piling soil into a bank in a sunny position. If your soil isn't free-draining, mix in some sand or gravel. Keep some of the bank free of weeds and other vegetation to allow the bees easy access. Some species live in wood, so adding a few logs with holes drilled in them will offer more than one type of home.

May

May is the last month when spring still prevails before the summer really gets under way. Wildflower meadows are blooming, the first garden roses are coming into flower and there is a delicious feeling of the days becoming perceptibly longer each evening. Baby birds are emerging from their nests and it seems the whole of nature is bursting with fresh life.

May

BY MAY THE WEATHER is hot enough for sitting in the garden with the warm air on bare skin, watching the first roses coming into bloom. The evenings are drawing out and at dusk the swooping flight of a house martin heading for its nest under the eaves is shortly replaced by bats hunting insects in the night air. Swifts have now arrived from Africa, their characteristic screaming calls announcing their presence as they wheel overhead; apart from the breeding season, these astonishing birds remain constantly airborne, even when they are asleep.

This is the month when you are most likely to have the privilege of hearing the glorious, melancholy song of the nightingale. Just arrived from Africa, the males are defending a territory and attracting a mate. Though they are famed for singing at night, they sometimes sing all day too and you may catch sight of a small, plain brown bird about the size of a thrush, its throat throbbing as it pours out its heart-stopping song. Nightingales are chiefly heard in Kent, Sussex, Essex and Suffolk but are found in other southern counties. If you live further north than an imaginary line from the Severn to the Wash, you will need to travel to hear them; Fingringhoe Wick, Essex Wildlife Trust's reserve on the west shore of the Colne Estuary, has the highest density in the UK. It will be worth the trip.

Many British resident birds are now coaxing their nestlings out into the world on unpractised wings, and you will see the parents darting from bush to bush as they feed their now scattered offspring; even harder work than their constant flight to and from a nestful of hungrily gaping beaks. Young mammals too are out and about, and you may catch sight of a litter of fox cubs engaged in mock fights as they exercise developing muscles and begin to learn the business of finding their own food.

The white, starry flowers of wild strawberries are now appearing, and in woodlands the brilliant blue of bugle is replacing the dying colour of bluebells. Red campion is flowering along shady lanes, with the flowers of white campion opening in

A male nightingale, Luscinia megarhynchos, *sits on a branch and sings*

the evening to attract the night-flying moths that will pollinate it. Above them the hawthorn comes gloriously into bloom this month, with hedgerows painting snowy lines across the landscape. In fact, with our warming climate, the blossom is sometimes well under way in April, but linked as it is with our May Day celebrations (see page 42) and with Shakespeare's description of it as 'the darling buds of May', it seems that it will always be regarded as a May-blooming plant no matter how much our seasons change.

Hawthorn has been used for hedging since ancient times, appearing in Anglo-Saxon boundary charters as haegthorn, 'haeg' being the Anglo-Saxon word for hedge. Much mythology and folklore is attached to it: Christ's crown of thorns is thought to have been hawthorn, as was St Joseph of Arimathea's staff. According to legend, when the saint thrust the staff into the ground on his passage through the English west country, it rooted and grew into the Glastonbury Thorn, a tree considered miraculous because it flowered for a second time in midwinter. Though the original was destroyed by Cromwell's troops, the custom of sending a budded branch to the Queen at Christmas has persisted from the time of Queen Anne to the present day.

If you wish to support wildlife in your garden, planting a hawthorn hedge is a major way of doing it: once established and of good thickness, it will provide a home for about 150 insect species, a nesting site for blackbirds and finches, and a source of food with its berries, or haws. The best species to choose for the garden is *Crataegus monogyna*, since the flowers of the other British native hawthorn, *Crataegus laevigata* (Midland hawthorn), smell of rotting flesh. In the wild, when the trees are in bloom your nose will tell you which is which without any doubt; at other seasons, you can tell the difference between them from the three lobes on the leaves of *Crataegus laevigata* as opposed to the five or seven leaves on *Crataegus monogyna*.

INTERNATIONAL DAWN CHORUS DAY

By May the dawn chorus is at its peak, with the resident birds now joined by all the migrants from the south. The purpose of bird song is to defend territory and attract a mate, and birds put their main effort into singing before daylight fully arrives. This is partly because the sound carries further on the still, quiet air and partly because there is not yet enough light to find food, which constitutes the main daily activity for birds.

International Dawn Chorus Day is held on the first Sunday in May, and you can observe it by joining in a dawn bird walk organized by your local wildlife trust, or by getting up at 4 a.m. to hear the dawn chorus from your window. You can find details on events in your area at www.idcd.info. Alternatively, if you really aren't good at early mornings, you can listen to it on BBC radio later in the day, recorded all over the world. You may also like to record it yourself. Though the sound quality wouldn't be good enough for a professional, for home enjoyment a minidisc recorder is ideal as it is so light and easy to slip into a pocket. If you invest in a decent microphone, costing £100 or so, you will be able to pick up sounds over quite a long distance.

Making a Herb Garden

A HERB GARDEN CAN BE as large or as small as you choose to make it, and if you are very short of space just a few containers or a windowsill will provide you with sufficient herbs to flavour your cooking. The only proviso is that you must have a sunny spot, since many herbs originate from the Mediterranean and were brought to Britain by the Romans.

The first formal herb gardens in Britain, and indeed throughout Europe, were created in monasteries, for monks acted as healers to the local population. Although the monks used herbs for culinary purposes, the prime reason for growing them was for their medicinal properties – a hit-and-miss affair while experimental use proved what worked and what didn't.

The nineteen-volume *Liber de Proprietatibus Rerum* (On the Properties of Things), written around 1230–1240 by a Franciscan monk, Bartholomaeus Anglicus (Bartholomew the Englishman), became the accepted reference work for the natural sciences for more than 200 years, translated from Latin into French, Spanish, Dutch and English. Although it dispelled the long-held notion that cinnamon was shot from the phoenix's nest with leaden arrows, the author informed his readership that the heliotrope 'with certain enchantments, doth beguile the sight of men that look thereon, and maketh a man that beareth it not to be seen'. Written in simple terms to be understood by less educated village preaching friars, the encyclopaedia had to be copied by scribes in commercial scriptoria or in monasteries. After Johann Gutenberg invented the European printing press in the fifteenth century the encyclopaedia gained even wider currency, with ten editions published. Now, in the twenty-first century, it is available in yet another incarnation with an even wider reach; it is published online with free access by the admirable Project Gutenberg (www.gutenberg.org).

Monastery herb gardens also contained vegetables and fruit and probably acted as a forerunner of the potager (see pages 56–57). The herb garden with four-square design, popular through many centuries to the present day, derives from the gardens of large churches, where the four beds originally represented the four rivers of paradise.

The four parts of the design may be rectangles, squares, circles or triangles, often with some type of pool in the centre.

If you decide to go for this relatively formal construction, draw out a design before you start digging and planting; using graph paper will help you to square up the design as you translate it to the garden. You will need to bear in mind the available sunlight and how your design will fit in with the

A formal herb garden in full bloom is attractive, as well as being a useful source of flavours

surrounding plants and garden structures. Obviously, you will want it to be near the house so that you can easily step out and pick a handful of herbs for the cooking pot and you will need pathways for easy access.

Most herbs need a well-drained soil. If yours isn't, raised beds solve the problem. Indeed, these are popular in any case as it is less far to bend to pick the herbs. Enclose them with brick, timber or, particularly attractive in a country garden, wattle fencing. Then it's just a matter of putting in your favourite herbs – perhaps lavender for its scent, peppermint for tea, basil for pesto and tomato salads, sage and rosemary for meat dishes, borage for adding a cucumber flavour to cool summer drinks and thyme for almost everything.

DRYING HERBS

Gather herbs for drying just before the flowers come out, after which time they lose a little of the flavour. Early in the morning on a fine day, after the dew has burnt off, cut perennials about one-third down the stem and annuals at ground level. Pick off any debris or decayed leaves. Tie woody-stemmed species in loose bunches and hang them up to dry in a shed or in the open – if the latter you will need to bring them in at night to protect them from dew. Place short-stemmed herbs and leaves such as sage in single layers on a wire rack to allow air to circulate and thus prevent mould forming. If it is the seeds you want, hang the herbs upside down inside a paper bag so that the seeds will fall into it.

For speed, you can dry herbs in the oven, taking care not to overheat them and thus damage their colour. Set the oven to its lowest heat, place the herbs on a flat baking sheet and leave them in the oven with the door open for two to four hours. If you have a microwave, an even quicker option is to put the herbs on a paper towel and microwave them for up to three minutes, mixing them every thirty seconds.

When the herbs are dry, store them in airtight containers. For maximum flavour, store the leaves whole and crumble them just before use. However, it is more convenient in terms of the space they take up to crumble the leaves between your fingers or rub them through a sieve before storing. Seeds should always be stored whole and ground when needed.

The Merriest Month

THOUGH LATE FROSTS are still a possibility, the beginning of May marks the time when the lengthening days and the fecundity of the countryside really lift the spirits. The increasing warmth of the weather tells us that winter is now really past and we can look forward to all the pleasures summer brings.

And if it is a relief to us now, with our centrally heated homes and choice of waterproof clothes, imagine how much more eagerly May was welcomed when the sole heating in a cottage was an open fire round which drenched clothes had to be dried out.

May Day

It's no wonder that the coming of May is regarded as a cause for much celebration. Traditionally, May Day was a time for setting out to gather greenery and flowers, especially May blossom from the hawthorn tree. Known as 'going a-maying', or 'bringing in the may', the celebration was associated with a good deal of goings-on between lads and maids in the woods: 'Many a green-gown has been given/Many a kiss, both odd and even', wrote the seventeenth-century poet Robert Herrick in *Corinna's Going A-Maying*, the 'green gown' referring to the consequences of a girl lying down in the grass with a young man. On a sterner note, the sixteenth-century critic Philip Stubbes wrote disapprovingly, 'of fortie, threescore or a hundred maides going to the wood over night, there have been scarecely the third part of them returned home againe undefiled.'

By the nineteenth century, the bawdier aspects of going a-maying

The ancient ritual of dancing round the maypole is now experiencing a revival in the countryside

The Green Man

In Christian centres all over Britain there appears, carved in stone or wood, the head of a man wreathed with foliage, sometimes peering through it, sometimes eating or disgorging it, and on occasion merging with it to create a strange half-human, half vegetative figure. Known here as 'the Green Man' he is not restricted to Britain; similar foliate heads can also be found in many European countries and in Turkey, India and Malaysia.

The origin of the Green Man is not known, but it seems certain that he long pre-dated Christianity and was subsequently incorporated into it, along with other pagan symbols and rituals that encouraged people to accept the new religion. He may have been a Celtic fertility god, a tree spirit that represents the vegetation so necessary to life on this planet, or he may symbolize the endless cycle of death and rebirth in nature and, in a Christian context, the death and resurrection of Christ; he is often to be found close to scenes of the Creation, Incarnation, Passion and Resurrection.

In his more pagan manifestations, the Green Man is also seen as a lord of misrule and appears as Jack-in-the-Green, or Jack o' Green. In the nineteenth century he was represented at May Day revels by a man inside a wicker frame covered with leaves who formed the centrepiece of a rowdy dance to the sound of drums and whistles. Today, with our increasing realization of our dependence on nature, the Green Man is experiencing something of a revival and you may find Jack o' Green present at May Day celebrations in your local town or village

---

were replaced by children going from house to house with garlands, collecting money in exchange for songs. There would usually be a May Queen, and perhaps other members of this extemporized May court such as maids of honour, pages and a king. The May Queen seems to be one of those traditions we just don't want to give up, as she still appears in many processions today.

Dancing round the maypole

The custom of decorating a maypole appears in literary references dating from as far back as the fourteenth century, and it formed an important focal point for community merrymaking to celebrate the coming of spring. In some places the maypole was a permanent fixture, while in others the business of erecting it started afresh each year.

However, such jollifications as dancing round a maypole were considered ungodly by many of the clergy and local judiciary, and once the Puritans came to power in the 1640s they were swiftly banned. Upon the Restoration, the high spirits the maypoles evoked made them a symbol of the new freedom from a dour and repressive period, and they came back into favour.

Over the centuries the custom of maypoling fell into decline, to be revived by the Victorians, who were much given to restoring, or indeed inventing, quaint British customs. Where once the maypoles had been garlanded with greenery, flowers and flags, now they gained ribbons, held by dancers, usually children, who weaved their way round the maypole, plaiting the ribbons around its trunk as they went. Today, a few villages still have maypoles, some even the pre-Victorian ribbonless variety.

Although such customs were declining by the 1960s, by the end of the century there was increased interest in our heritage and today maypole dancing in particular is gaining in popularity. If you like the idea of taking part in a dance, or perhaps would like to hold one in your community, see page 94 for further information.

June

June is the month of long twilights, hot summer days and the feeling that the whole world is pulsing with new growth and energy. The young foliage on the trees is still a fresh, bright green, untouched as yet by the dust and heat of full summer; in our gardens, roses are bursting gloriously into bloom. It's no wonder that, for many people, this is the best month of all.

June

IN JUNE, THE DAYS are so long and the nights so short that, in fine weather, it can be hard to get enough sleep. The fresh, sparkling dawns and long golden evenings are so delicious that the temptation is to cut down on hours spent in bed so as not to miss anything going on outside. While there is still plenty of summer to come, the days will slowly start drawing in again – after the longest day on the summer Solstice, 21 June – and there is something special about being able to sit outside and read in the twilight until nearly 10 p.m.

There is a plethora of things to see and do at this time of year, too. Sit beside a countryside pond or river for a while – you may find it edged yellow with native irises among the rushes – and you will see electric blue damselflies and dragonflies darting to and fro above the surface, or an even brighter flash of colour from a family of kingfishers, their first brood out and about on the wing. Walk in sunlit woodland and you will find foxgloves in flower, growing perhaps at the shady base of an old fallen tree. In open ground, skylarks will be singing above your head and a few fields that have escaped herbicides will be red with poppies. To add to the explosion of colour, others may be swathed in the gorgeous violet blue of flax, a plant which was cultivated in Britain as long ago as 700BC and is now an increasingly popular crop with farmers for its seeds (linseed) and fibre.

Elder trees are coming into bloom now, their profuse creamy-

Elderflower begins to blossom at this time of year: it is a wonderful source of flavour, lending a subtle taste to food and drink alike

Elderflower fritters

- pancake batter (see page 17)
- 2–3 elderflowers per person, with stalks
- butter or oil for frying
- sugar, honey, lemon juice or syrup, to serve

Make the batter as described on page 17 then, holding the elderflowers by the stalks, dip them into the batter. Allow the batter to drain off a little then dip the elderflowers into the butter or oil until golden brown. Serve with sugar, honey, lemon juice or syrup to taste.

Elderflower cordial

- 20 elderflower heads, stalks removed
- 1 lemon, sliced
- 2tsp citric acid
- 1.5kg (3$\frac{1}{2}$lb) sugar
- 1.2 ltrs (2$\frac{1}{2}$pt) boiling water

Place the elderflowers, lemon, citric acid and sugar in a bucket and pour the boiling water over them. Stir until the sugar has dissolved and skim off any scum. Cover the bucket with a cloth and leave for five days, stirring twice a day.

Strain the cordial through muslin or a fine sieve and pour into sterilized bottles with screw tops. Keep in the refrigerator. Dilute to taste with water as with other cordials.

white flowerheads unmissable. Both the flowers and the berries are popular for making a variety of drinks such as wine, 'champagne', beer and cordial, and elderflower fritters make a tasty snack. (Though be warned that neither the flowers nor the berries should be eaten raw as they contain a poison, which is destroyed by cooking.) Ideally, pick elderflowers for edible purposes on a warm, dry day; don't take them from roadside trees, as they will be heavily polluted from car exhausts.

You will find it harder to spot the less blatant flowers of wild orchids, but this is the month to go looking for them. There are about fifty native species, some rare and endangered, others relatively common. You are most likely to discover them in marshy areas, in woodland or on chalk or limestone downland, depending on the species; as they tend to like poor soils, you are unlikely to see them on agricultural land.

While resident birds' first brood have left the nest (and they may be well on the way with a second), migratory birds such as swallows have only recently hatched their eggs. You may find a pair have commandeered a spot in your outbuildings or garage, and you will see the flash of their wings as they swoop at high speed to their nest. If the entrance to the building is just a small crevice it can be heartstopping to see them approach it at such speed, but their agility and precision is such that they will be through it and inside almost before you have really registered their approach.

Fruit is ripening on wild cherries now, and you will see a range of birds including pigeons, blackbirds and thrushes feasting on it. Small green sloes are appearing on blackthorn, promising a chance to make sloe gin later in the year (see page 79), and the hedgerows are swagged with the creamy flowers of travellers' joy twined with dog roses and wild honeysuckle. Though every month of the year has interest and beauty, it's hard to beat June for sheer abundance of choice.

The Name of a Rose

ROSES MUST BE the most well-loved flowers in the British psyche; they appear again and again in poetry, prose and art, and carry a powerful symbolism. It has not always been easy, though, to incorporate them into a cottage garden, or one where the overall feeling is of naturalism. In municipal spaces, roses occupy bare beds, with stark, stiff stems and branches carefully pruned. For those who like the formal style, this type of rose cultivation is ideal. For informality and rustic charm, it doesn't work.

After the Second World War, new rose varieties in vibrant colours with modern names such as 'Majorette' became the fashion. In the fifties, garden centres – a new concept from the USA – presented roses in serried ranks of containers which were snapped up in their thousands: 'man-made' was in and natural was out. Novice gardeners could now buy plants as easily as baked beans, without having to locate specialized nurseries where plants had to be ordered in advance, and then arrived bare-rooted, requiring some thought as to how they should be planted. Only aficionados of old rose types knew where to find the roses celebrated by the poets.

By the 1980s, though, the pendulum was beginning to swing back and the nurseries that had stuck by the old-fashioned roses found their loyalty rewarded, with newcomers springing up and raising the profile of these plants still further. Now, a good garden centre will have a selection of them and it is certainly convenient to be able to buy them

container-grown to plant at any time of year. For real romance and a much bigger choice, though, obtain catalogues from the specialists and enjoy reading details of each rose; you will probably find you end up with a shortlist of twenty or more and spend a few painful hours whittling that down further. You won't receive your rose until the dormant season – perhaps Christmas or even later if the winter has been mild – but if you leave ordering until the autumn you may find the plants you want have all been taken.

Choosing your roses

Roses are very tolerant plants and although they prefer a clay soil they will grow almost anywhere; consequently, your decisions mainly rest on colour, scent and scale. The reason the old-fashioned shrub roses blend so well into a mixed border is that their colours are gentle and their growth less stiff and formal than the modern rose. Consider the colour and height of other plants in your border and you will find a rose that will be a good companion to them.

If you study rose catalogues and books you will not find complete unanimity about the date that divides old roses from modern ones, but unless you want to be purist about it this is not something to worry about. There is also a category called English roses, bred since the 1970s, which combine the appearance of old roses with improved disease resistance: organic gardeners who don't wish to spray their roses may find these a better option, though it's possible by careful cultivation to keep disease to a minimum. In any case, gardeners who have fallen in love with old roses tend to be so focused on the beauty of the flowers that they regard some blackspot as little to worry about; certainly Gertrude Jekyll and Vita Sackville-West, who revived interest in old roses in an earlier age, were not deterred by it. The pleasure and romance of growing a rose that was a favourite of Josephine de Beauharnais in her garden at Malmaison more than makes up for a few flaws. However, the English roses do also have the advantage of repeat flowering while most of the old roses give you one glorious flush of flowers and then it's all over until the following year.

As well as planting roses in the border, choose climbers and ramblers for your house walls or your trees – but check first on their habit. 'Albertine' is a glorious salmon-pink rambler with thorns so vicious it makes an excellent burglar deterrent, but will also cause you problems if you place it so that you have to brush past it; while *Rosa filipes* 'Kiftsgate', with creamy-white

'Ferdinand Prichard' has crimson-striped petals and a strong, rich fragrance

flowers, can be overwhelmingly vigorous for a small garden as it can reach 15m (50ft). 'Zéphirine Drouhin', a climber with masses of very fragrant pink flowers, will do well on a north wall or as a hedge, and is completely thornless, so is a good rose to choose if you have small children. Having access to such information is the advantage of buying from a specialist rose nursery rather than impulse buying from a garden centre.

Given the longevity of roses, they are really very inexpensive to buy compared to the cost of bedding plants; they are generally about the price of a moderately good bottle of wine, which is gone in an evening. If a rose turns out not to be as pleasing in terms of fragrance or appearance as you had hoped from the catalogue description (such things are after all subjective), just decide to dispense with it and order another variety, replacing the soil to avoid disease if you are planting in the same spot. It's also worth taking a deliberate risk here and there; the simple, blush-pink rose 'Souvenir de St Anne's', for example, looks nothing particularly special in a catalogue photograph and may even be listed without one, but the fragrance is so glorious that you will probably order more as soon as you have experienced it. It is also worth paying a June visit to notable rose gardens for inspiration, such as Mottisfont Abbey at Romsey, Hampshire, and the restored Victorian rose garden at Warwick Castle, near Coventry.

Finally, choose supports for your roses that look old or natural, rather than modern plastic ones. A woven hazel arch will blend beautifully with a climber, as will reclaimed old railing. If your roses are in an enclosed area, making a simple gate from coppiced poles nailed to each other horizontally and vertically will give the entrance a rustic, wonky charm.

ROSE PETAL JELLY

- 450ml (3/4pt) water
- 2 large teacupfuls of pink rose petals, tightly packed
- 500g (1lb 2oz) sugar
- 60ml (2fl oz) lemon juice
- 75g (3oz) packet liquid pectin

Place the water in a medium-sized pan and bring to the boil. Remove from the heat, add the petals and leave to steep for 30 minutes. Strain the water into a fresh saucepan and discard the petals.

Add the sugar and lemon juice to the pan, mix well and bring to the boil, stirring constantly. Boil for 2 minutes, add the pectin and boil for a further 2 minutes. Remove from the heat, skim off any foam with a metal spoon and pour into sterilized jars. Leave to cool completely then store in the refrigerator for up to six months.

Salads with a Difference

IF YOU GROW YOUR own salad leaves you'll have food on the table that beats supermarket produce into a cocked hat in terms of freshness and flavour. There's nothing quite like the taste of leaves that were still growing the same day you eat them, and the powerful fragrance of a freshly picked lettuce is long gone by the time it's been put in a plastic bag and trucked across the country.

So if you have the space, you'll really benefit from growing most of your own salad vegetables. If your garden is very small or you are short of time, the best plan is to cultivate those varieties that are hard to obtain in the shops. Many of the more unusual salad leaves, for example, can only be bought in pricey mixed packs; you may also not like the fact that they have been washed in chlorine bleach.

Cos lettuce is easily available from grocers and supermarkets, but lettuces are heavily sprayed with pesticides – the reason why you often see just the hearts on sale. That alone makes them worth allocating some space for. To add colour, grow some rusty-red 'Lollo Rosso' or some red oak leaf lettuce such as 'Mascara' or 'Red Feuille de Chêne'. The leaves of 'Flame' turn cherry red in the centre as they grow, while those of 'Pablo' are overlaid with dark purple. 'Australian Yellowleaf', a large open-headed lettuce with bright yellow-green leaves, will contrast nicely.

Green and purple orache grows quickly early in the year, with spinach-like leaves tasting rather like butterhead lettuce. To grow watercress you will need a very shady, damp bed and preferably a stream, but land cress is more versatile and

has a similarly spicy, hot flavour. If you like some bitterness in your salads, grow radicchio, chicory and endive; Belgian chicory, the vegetable that looks not unlike a huge tulip bud, will require blanching or it will be unpleasantly bitter. Confusingly, in France this is called endive and what we call curly endive is chicory frisée, so you may sometimes see curly endive labelled frisée on British market stalls.

Rocket (or roquette) is expensive to buy but grows very fast and is very tolerant as to soil and site. It is a hardy annual and can withstand a mild winter. Pick the leaves while they are young. As it runs to seed quickly in hot weather, sow it frequently in small quantities.

Salsola has crisp, thin leaves and is easy to grow. Gather it in bunches when young and eat it raw in salads for its salty, crunchy taste and texture, or boil it and eat it as a vegetable. Corn salad, or lamb's lettuce, will give you fresh leaves in winter when no lettuce is available; sow in late spring for a summer crop or in late summer for winter leaves.

You will rarely see leaf sorrel for sale and this is a mystery, as the lemony flavour is a real asset to a salad. It is so easy to grow that you could leave it in a container and forget to water it for weeks, only to find that it forgives you and regrows once given the basic necessities of a plant's life. It also makes fabulous soup.

You won't often find fresh borlotti beans for sale in the UK, and they are well worth growing for their decorative appearance as well as their flavour when eaten fresh rather than dried. Their red and white flecked pods add unusual colour. Try also Purple King beans, which are so dark as to be almost black. Cooked, they are delicious cold or warm.

ORIENTAL VEGETABLES

Our salads today are often enlivened by Oriental vegetables, which were largely unknown on the British table twenty years ago. The giant Japanese mooli radish, which can grow up to 30cm (12in) long, is very fast-growing and can be grated

into a salad or added to a stir-fry just a few weeks after sowing. Just as obliging are the Oriental brassicas: growing them as a cut-and-come-again crop is easy. Pak choi is delicious raw in salads and steamed, braised or stir-fried; mizuna will grow in both summer and winter, its pretty foliage adding a decorative element, and will add a mustard flavour to salads and other dishes; komatsuna, or spinach mustard, is reminiscent of cabbage and spinach. For Chinese cabbage, choose the variety 'Santo' for a good cut-and-come-again crop.

Oriental brassicas don't like to be transplanted; sow them directly or in modules. They are more shallow-rooted than the typical British brassicas, so be sure to keep them well watered at this time of year or they will dry out and run to seed. You can expect to be eating pak choi within about six weeks, komatsuna and Chinese cabbage after eight weeks, mizuna after about ten and Oriental mustards in six to thirteen weeks.

Growing your own lettuces means you can be more in control of your exposure to pesticides. From left: curly endive, lollo rosso, cos, lamb's lettuce, butterhead lettuce, frisée and radicchio

July

July is the month when the holidays begin and everyone wants a taste of the outdoor life. The growing season is reaching its apex and most new animal families are now out and about, the young able to fend for themselves. On hot days, it seems the whole countryside is replete and drowsy with well-being.

July

JULY IS HIGH SUMMER, when tree canopies are in glorious full leaf. Children make the most of their holidays and adults, too, head for the garden whenever weather and time allow. A seemingly unending supply of salad leaves rewards the small effort of sowing a few packets of seed earlier in the year, and there's the joy of wandering outside to gather the contents of a summery meal just yards from your door, putting them on the table within the hour when they have barely stopped growing. Even the best organic vegetables from a shop cannot compare with the energetic taste of food this fresh, while soft fruit varieties, grown for their flavour rather than for their supermarket eye-appeal, are a revelation.

Water for the garden can be a real problem at this time of year, particularly in light of the increasing frequency of hosepipe bans – depending on where you live, of course. One of the best ways to get around this problem is to buy a water butt. This can then sit, discreetly tucked away beneath the down-pipe of a gutter, allowing you to dip in your watercan or run the water out of the tap on the side. It should provide you with a reserve of water, hopefully throughout the year.

In the countryside the fields lie golden with corn, edged with blue scabious and purple knapweed, and the hedgerows bloom with willowherb, yarrow and other wild flowers. Once, these fields would have provided homes for thousands of harvest mice, their nests woven between the stalks, but these have retreated from the advance of the combine harvester and you are most likely to find them now in reeds and thistles. The latter are also in demand by goldfinches, which love their seeds; you may think it worth having a prickly

SUMMER PUDDING

Serves 6

This classic English pudding is a well-loved part of the summer menu, best eaten outdoors with sunshine sparkling on an accompanying glass of dessert white wine. You can combine strawberries, raspberries, redcurrants, blackcurrants and blackberries, but use the latter in moderation as their flavour and colour will dominate if you are not careful. This dish looks best a glorious crimson colour.

- 6–8 slices of day-old white bread, crusts removed
- 675g (1½lb) soft fruits, washed and hulled
- 125–150g (4–5oz) caster sugar
- whipped cream, to serve

Line a 900ml (1½pt) pudding basin with the bread, trimming the slices if necessary to fit the sides and reserving sufficient for a lid. Put the fruit in a heavy-based saucepan, sprinkle the sugar over it and heat for 2 minutes or until the sugar dissolves and the juice runs. Pour the fruit into the bowl and cover with the reserved bread. Place a plate over the top and weight it down, then chill the pudding for 8 hours. Turn out onto a plate and serve with cream.

Foliage Dens

Children love outdoor dens for the sense these give of having a little place of their own where they can hide away. Building them one which is covered with foliage adds extra enchantment, as the leaves spread day by day to make it more secret, and then begin to turn russet by the end of summer.

An easy way to create a den is to make a wigwam of tall poles, thrust into the ground in a circle and tied together at the top (see the illustration opposite). It's best to start off with five or so poles to establish the shape and then fill in with more. Attaching two or three horizontal poles between two of them will give you a structure on which to tie up stems so that a doorway is left clear. Planting a vine such as *Vitis coignetiae* or *Vitis vinifera* 'Brandt' will give the children luxuriant cover; the former variety will offer glorious autumn colour, the latter a less spectacular autumn display but bunches of sweet black grapes – except that blackbirds will find them palatable before you do and you will be lucky to have any left to ripen fully.

Living willow structures are popular, and it's easy to make a den or tunnel by erecting stems in the shape you wish to achieve. Plant willow stems between November and March in a trench about 30 cm (1 ft) deep, with plenty of organic matter added. Water well and watch the bare stems burst into growth in spring.

plant or two in the garden to attract them, so you can admire the gold flash of their wings.

Having raised their young, birds such as robins, thrushes and blackbirds are ceasing to sing and going into moult, but the chirping of the meadow cricket now provides background music for sunny days. One of the most charming sights you will see in a sunny garden is a blackbird sunbathing, wings spread out and head tilted, beak agape. Families of tits and finches are out and about together, descending *en masse* on trees to feed off insects and seeds, while on lakes and rivers you will see a solemn procession of dowdy grey-brown cygnets paddling behind their majestic parents. Summer is here, and it seems for a few short weeks that nature is on 'pause' while we make the most of it.

With less intensive farming practices, we are beginning to see cornflowers and other native wildflowers re-emerging in the fields

Making a Potager

WITH THE INCREASED public interest in garden design, many people want a vegetable plot that is more than utilitarian in appearance and the decorative potager is increasingly popular. The idea of formal beds of flowers, vegetables and herbs dates from medieval times and if you wish to delve into historical advice on creating a potager, William Lawson's two books, *A New Orchard and Garden* and *The Country Housewife's Garden* are a good source. A parish priest in Yorkshire, Lawson was an enthusiastic gardener and several centuries ahead of his time in his environmental concerns and his championship of women's employment. Published originally in 1618, the books are now available in a single facsimile edition from Prospect Books.

However, if the formal style of geometric designs often enclosed by box hedging is not for you, there is nothing to stop you making a more informal and romantic potager – an increasing trend in France, where this style is known as the *jardin de curé* (country curate's garden). Here there are flowers in greater abundance, typically simple and traditional species both perennial and annual, such as cosmos (*Cosmos*), nasturtiums (*Tropaeolum majus*), marigolds (*Tagetes*), sweetpeas (*Lathyrus odoratus*) and hollyhocks (*Alcea*). Yet still there are plenty of pathways that create divisions through the potager, for the essence of growing your own food is that it must be easy to cultivate and harvest.

Think first of all about the design as a whole and how it will suit the space you can allocate to it before you design the individual beds. It's practical to make the main paths wide enough to take a wheelbarrow, and to make sufficient paths to avoid treading on the beds to reach your vegetables, as this will compact the soil and create more work for you. To edge your beds, low wattle fencing or weathered old bricks are both less

Exploring the Style

To create a particular garden style, there's nothing like visiting other gardens to see different interpretations. You will not only absorb the underlying principles of what you are trying to achieve but also derive ideas of how you can use your favourite plants and adapt, if need be, to suit your soil conditions and climate.

To find the type of garden you are looking for, check out the National Gardens Scheme website, www.ngs.org.uk. The NGS has organized the opening of gardens to the public for more than seventy-five years, with entrance charges going to charity. Most are private gardens open for just a few days a year, though some are accessible to the public on a commercial basis. The gardens are listed in a handbook originally called *The Gardens of England and Wales*, though the brilliant yellow cover caused it to be universally known as 'The Yellow Book', under which title it is now sold. For going out and about in an unfamiliar area the book is indispensable, but if you are looking for a special feature such as a potager you can search the excellent website, where you will find more than sixty gardens with potagers listed.

Perhaps the most famous potager of all is that at the sixteenth-century Château Villandry, 20km (14 miles) west of Tours, in France. The gardens were laid out in the early twentieth century to sixteenth-century geometric designs, with the potager comprising nine squares, each with its own beautiful colour scheme. Villandry is included on every garden tour of France, but really keen gardeners make for it during the *Journées du Potager* in autumn, when the public can meet the team of gardeners and benefit from their expertise.

In the UK, the best-known potager was probably the one at Barnsley House, near Cirencester, Gloucestershire, part of the glorious gardens created by the late Rosemary Verey. Barnsley House is now a hotel and, other than to guests, the gardens are open to the public only occasionally but you can still read Rosemary Verey's account of it in her book *The Making of a Garden* (Frances Lincoln, 1995). Her wonderful design was based upon the Potager du Roi at Versailles, created by Jean Baptiste La Quintinie for Louis XIV between 1678 and 1683 and barely altered since.

Cornucopias of delight – potagers provide visual as well as edible enjoyment

formal than smartly clipped box hedging. If you have a brick house or garden wall, brick edging and paths will make the potager sit comfortably within its location.

You will need to introduce vertical accents such as small fruit trees or poles of tomatoes or beans. When you are choosing your vegetables, make a point of deciding on varieties that have attractively coloured leaves: red and russet lettuces, ruby chard, blue-green kale, yellow courgettes and red cabbage will give a stunning display. Within the fixed structures of your paths, you can vary the design of the planting from season to season, choosing triangles, squares or straight rows as the fancy takes you. After you have harvested crops, sow fast-growing, cut-and-come-again salad greens to fill the spaces, or green manures such as mustard (*Brassica*) and phacelia (*Phacelia tanacetifolia*) which will look attractive growing and then nurture the soil when dug into it.

A pergola or arbour will provide more structure and height to your potager. Vines or hops make suitably productive plants to climb up them, or you may prefer something that will leave the frame more visible, such as a climbing rose. If you want to make your own structure and are not too sure of your carpentry skills, you can rely on the plants to hide your mistakes during the summer months when you are most likely to be lingering in the potager.

On the Hoof

IF YOU HAVE A SMALL paddock, or indeed a garden bigger than your urge to cultivate it that could be partly turned over to fenced land, you may find yourself with the feeling that it should have some inhabitants. Unless you have ambitions to be a farmer you won't want the trouble of milking a cow, and a horse would require lots of decent space, regular exercise and not inconsiderable expenditure. So how about angora goats or alpacas, which can fulfil multiple roles as friendly pets, suppliers of manure for the garden and providers of fleece?

Angora goats

Angoras are an ancient breed that descended from a Central Asian species, and their hair was used for clothing many centuries BC. They were taken to Turkey in the eleventh or twelfth century but were not known at all in Europe until the mid-sixteenth century, when a pair was given to the Pope. However, their fleece was so highly prized that for several centuries exportation of either fleece or animal from Turkey was banned.

Angoras first arrived in the UK in the early 1980s, imported with the idea that farmers would make a more than healthy income from their fleece, or mohair. For a time, high prices were paid for the animals, but as reality dawned excitement faded and eventually an equilibrium was established with a number of dedicated producers managing herds of varying sizes. Today, you can buy a pedigree female Angora from £100 or, if you are not fussy about bloodlines, £50 will acquire you one of these friendly and gentle beasts. You will need to buy at least two, though, because they are herd animals and it would be cruel to condemn one to a solitary life. A quarter of an acre will provide sufficient space for a pair.

Although they have less tendency than dairy goats to make an escape bid, you will still need a decent stock fence and some shelter for them, especially during the winter and after they have been shorn in the spring if the season is a cold and wet one. They will be delighted to graze their way through brambles, nettles and thistles but if you plan to use their fleece, a muddy pasture is not ideal. Their needs aren't complicated, but include fresh water daily, supplemental feeding and foot trimming. As with any animals, take the trouble to learn about their care and welfare before you acquire them to make sure you are able and willing to look after them properly; the British Angora Goat Society (see page 94) is your best source of information in this instance. The Society will also provide a directory of breeders and lists of local societies and shows.

Angoras are shorn of their fleece twice a year. As it grows 2.5cm (1in) a month, this means the six-month fleece is an ideal length for spinning. British mohair is highly regarded for its durability and softness, and you have several options as to what to do with it: sell it to a spinner (up to about £10 per 1kg, or $2^{1}/_{4}$lb), commission a spinner to spin it for you, or spin it yourself. Depending on your enthusiasm for traditional crafts, there can be immense satisfaction from producing your own fleece derived from an animal you have cared for, and then transforming it into wool, perhaps coloured with dyes from the vegetables in your garden. You will find spinners advertising their services in the classified section of most smallholding magazines.

Alpacas

Alpacas are somewhat larger than goats and a good deal more expensive to buy, but make charming, docile, affectionate pets. As with Angoras, you will need to have at least a pair.

From South America (mainly Peru, Bolivia and Chile), alpacas are from the same family as llamas, guanacos and vicunas, collectively known as New World Camelids. They were domesticated about 5,000 years ago and used for food, clothing and transport. Interestingly, recent archaeological discoveries show that the fibre of their fleece during the period of Inca civilization was of a higher quality

than is found in the present day. After the arrival of the Spanish Conquistadores in the sixteenth century and the destruction of the Inca empire, the carefully bred alpaca herds were dispersed to the higher elevations of the Andes to survive as they might.

The harsh nature of their native terrain means that alpacas regard the cold of a British winter with equanimity. However, because their fleece lacks lanolin (and is therefore hypoallergenic), in heavy rain it may become saturated. Consequently, you will need to provide a shelter so that you can take them inside if need be. They eat grass and hay, and you can also buy special alpaca food. As they will also happily browse any hedges you may have, you should take care that these do not contain poisonous plants.

The fleece, which is even finer than mohair, is shorn just once a year – unclipped, it will reach ground level. You can expect the shorn fleece to weigh 0.8–2.8 kg (1–6lb). Huaca alpacas, the hardiest type, have wavy fleeces, while Suri alpaca fleece has a silky texture; the fleece of Chili alpacas is somewhere in between the two in quality. Joining the British Camelids Association (see page 94) will give you access to breeders, welfare advice and workshops.

Clothing made from alpaca wool is becoming more and more popular as an alternative to sheep's wool, particularly as it is lanolin free

August

The beginning of August is high summer and there are holidays in the air, perhaps by the sea or in the depths of the green and golden countryside. But by the end of the month there's a definite feeling that every glorious hot day must be cherished, for the ones that remain may be counted on your fingers.

August

There's a certain poignancy to August, for it represents the last weeks of summer and all they bring: paddling in seaside rock pools, late-evening al fresco suppers in the fading light, and wildflowers and insect life at their peak before the year tilts slowly over into autumn and the different pleasures it brings. In estuaries, wading birds are arriving for a stopover on their way to the warmth of Africa, the earliest representatives of the great autumn migration that will shortly stir into life. Also on the shore are golden plovers, lapwings and dunlins, and as this is the time that wildfowl are going into moult you will probably find many discarded feathers that tell which birds have passed that way.

Inland, the harvesting of the grain crops has left fields with bare golden stubble and kestrels hover above them, looking for prey such as field voles which have lost their safe cover of tall stems. However, in only a very short time small wildflowers such as scarlet pimpernel and willowherb will quickly colonize the stubble and provide at least some new protection. Small field dwellers need it: birds of prey have extraordinarily powerful eyesight, and it is estimated that, given a kestrel's capabilities in this respect, we could read a newspaper at 22m (25yd). Not only that, they can pick up the scent of the urine and faeces with which rodents mark their runs so they can simply stay motionless in exactly the right spot above, poised to strike a scurrying form as soon as it appears. For people who have had infestations of house mice leaving odiferous trails across their kitchens, this may bring a certain grim satisfaction.

As the bright colours of many wildflowers are starting to vanish from the countryside, the hedgerows are beginning to glow with the red berries of hawthorn and guelder rose, interspersed with large clusters of black elderberries and orange dog rose hips. You will also spot the blue bloom of new sloe berries, promising the chance to make sloe gin next month. Blackberries are glossy and ripe, and even if you go out with the intention of collecting them for desserts it's impossible to resist sampling them as you go: perhaps one for the mouth to every three for the container? But don't succumb to the temptation to settle for easy pickings from roadside

Peacock

Blackberry and apple crumble
Serves 4–6

Plain flour is usually suggested for making crumbles, but if you feel like a heartier one, use wholewheat flour or a half-and-half mixture of flour and oatflakes – either porridge oats or, for extra texture, jumbo oats. This isn't a refined dessert: it's a good old-fashioned pud.

- 450g (1lb) cooking apples, peeled, cored and sliced
- 225g (8oz) blackberries, washed
- 75g (3oz) caster sugar

For the topping:
- 225g (8oz) flour
- 75g (3oz) butter
- 150g (5oz) soft brown sugar

Preheat the oven to 190°C/375°F/Gas mark 5. Combine the fruit in a 1.7 litre (3pt) pie dish.

To make the crumble, place the flour in a mixing bowl then cut in the butter and rub it into the flour with your fingertips until it is evenly dispersed and the mixture has a nice crumbly consistency. Add the sugar and mix well.

Spoon the crumble over the fruit, spreading it out evenly. Place the pie dish on a baking tray and bake in the oven for 35–45 minutes until the top is tinged golden.

Picking blackberries is a lovely way to get outside for fresh air, and have something to show for it at the end

hedgerows as these berries will be contaminated with fumes from the combustion engine, which is hardly what you want when collecting food from the wild.

As garden birds finish their moult, some begin to sing again, though in a desultory way compared to their spring song. Robins in particular, aggressive little birds that they are, sing to announce their winter territories with no apparent comprehension of their limitations; you can approach a robin's favoured bush with a whirring hedgetrimmer and find it perched on a fence or branch beside it, throat swelling with effort as it pours out what it perceives to be a daunting song to warn you off. Tits too are singing to defend territory, though they are both more circumspect and more sociable than robins, joining other tits in a hunt for food.

The early colours of autumn are beginning to tinge some trees, and after a breezy day you may find the first yellowing leaves scattered on your lawn. Silver birches are one of the first to turn, though they may keep many of their leaves until nearly Christmas. Though there are still many summery butterflies such as tortoiseshells and peacocks about at the beginning of the month, by its end there is an unmistakeable whiff of autumn as the sun begins to sink lower in the sky. There may still be warm days to come, but the summer has reached its end.

Late Summer Colour

IT IS EASY TO FILL the garden with a riot of colour in spring and early summer, but you need also to plan for late summer colour that will last through into autumn, or you will suddenly find the garden looking a bit drab. Happily, many of the later-flowering species are in fiery reds and bronzes, bringing heat to the garden just as it begins to ebb from the sun.

Dahlias are one of the most well-known plants for autumn colour and they are now coming back into favour after some years in the wilderness. Their flower heads range from tight pompoms to the shaggy heads of the cactus type, and are coloured white, cream, yellow, pink and a variety of reds and bronzes. Flowering from midsummer until the first frosts, they could solve the question of late colour without the help of any other genus at all. If you live in a frost-free area, you can leave the tubers in the ground over winter, otherwise lift them once the foliage has been blackened by frost, pack them in boxes of peat or dry sand and store in a well-ventilated place.

Salvias and penstemons will provide quieter spires of blue, lavender, purple and red, but if you want tall, upright shapes that will rival the dahlias for flamboyance, kniphofias (red hot pokers) may take your fancy. Again the colour range is warm, with reds and bronzes through to yellows and creams, many of them two-tone. Most of the available species are perennial in the UK.

Remember to include some plants that will leave interesting winter skeletons. Sedums have attractive glaucous leaves that set off pink, green and cream flowers. They are easy to grow in well-drained soil and a sunny spot, and they are favoured by bees and butterflies. *Sedum spectabile* 'Brilliant', with large pink flowerheads, is one of the best in this respect. *Sedum* 'Herbstfreude'

Big bold flowers such as dahlias can prolong the vibrant colours of summer well into autumn

Prairie gardens

With the increased interest in gardening with nature rather than against it, prairie gardens have become very fashionable and these come into their own in late summer and autumn. Here brightly coloured flowers of the daisy family mingle with ornamental grasses to give a natural effect that will bring colour and interest long into the year. Try rudbeckias in bronze, mahogany or yellow, some with flowers up to 15cm (6in) across; heleniums in similar colours, growing up to 1.8m (6ft) tall; and purple coneflowers (*Echinacea*).

For grasses to accompany them, pheasant grass (*Stipa arundinacea*) bears purple-green spikelets from midsummer to early autumn. They billow on mounds of orange-brown leaves, giving an effect somewhat like backcombed hair, and as this is a perennial evergreen grass the leaves will last all over winter. Pennisetums are another late summer and autumn-flowering grass with fluffy seedheads that will last until mid- or late winter; these need a well-drained soil throughout winter or they will not survive. The colours of the spikelets range from creamy-white through pink, violet, gold and purple.

Most grasses come in subtle shades, but one notable exception to the rule is the Japanese blood grass *Imperata cylindrica* 'Red Baron'. The young foliage is green with red tips that slowly flush down the blades, becoming a rich burgundy colour by autumn. With the setting sun behind it, the effect is stunning.

('Autumn Joy') is less popular with insects but very popular with humans, its flowers opening pink in early autumn and then mutating through pinkish-bronze to copper red. Leave the dead flowerheads on the stems, for they look wonderful rimed with frost.

Cardoons (*Cynara cardunculus*), thistle-like relatives of the globe artichoke, have a strongly architectural shape and purple early-summer to early-autumn flowers that turn into striking seedheads with silvery hairs, excellent for drying. Another good spiky contender for winter interest is sea holly (*Eryngium*). There are several species and varieties, one favourite being *Eryngium giganteum*, known as Miss Willmott's Ghost, named after the celebrated gardener Ellen Willmott, who had the slightly eccentric habit of scattering its seeds in her friends' gardens. The flowers are a steely blue, with silvery-grey bracts that suggest winter even before the frost sculpts their outlines yet further.

Drying flowers

Although there's no shortage of dried flowers on sale, it's satisfying to pick and dry flowers you have grown yourself to act as a reminder of days in the garden, even in the depths of winter. To air dry them, gather them when they are dry, divide them into small bunches and secure them with an elastic band (not string or wire, as the stems will shrink as they dry). Hang them upside down in a warm and airy room, preferably in the dark to avoid the colours fading.

Foliage (including grasses) is best dried using a solution of glycerine. Make this by mixing two parts of hot water to one part of glycerine, stirring well. Place the stems in warm water for at least a couple of hours, then transfer them to the glycerine solution while it is lukewarm. The foliage will usually change colour, but what shade this may be depends on the time of year you dry it. Remove the plants from the glycerine once you can see that the solution has been taken up to the veins at the top of the leaves.

A speedy way to dry flowers is in the microwave, though clearly you will be limited here as to size and stem length. Start by experimenting with low power and very short times – you will discover that varying them results in varying colours too. Remember, of course, not to tie the flowers with wire.

Growing Superfoods

SCIENTIFIC INVESTIGATIONS have recently discovered health-giving properties in some plants that have led to them being described as 'superfoods'. Among them are nuts, blueberries and cranberries, and gardeners are taking to cultivating them with enthusiasm.

Many people associate the growing of nuts with trees of a decent size, but walnuts and hazelnuts grow successfully in the UK in containers. So too do blueberries and cranberries, now much in demand for their curative qualities. Combine chopped nuts with handfuls of berries and some oat or wheat flakes and you will have delicious home-made muesli.

Blueberries

Ten years ago you'd be lucky to find blueberries (*Vaccinium corymbosum*) in even the most sophisticated supermarkets, but now they are a common sight. No doubt this is in large part because of the scientific studies that have found them not only to be of use in reducing cholesterol, preventing memory loss and improving sight, but also to be much higher in antioxidants than most other fruit and vegetables. However, many of the blueberries on sale are imported from countries with hotter climates than Britain and the flavour and texture are not as good as you will experience if you grow your own in cooler temperatures that suit them better.

In the USA, blueberries were first grown commercially from seedlings of wild blueberries which were popular with Native Americans. In the UK, their relative the bilberry, or blaeberry, grows on acidic soils on heaths, mountains and moors. There's nothing quite as good as discovering them amid the wild heather on top of a fell and eating them while contemplating a sublime view of distant peaks; but on a practical level, growing them in pots outside your kitchen door will give you a more reliable supply.

Of course, if you have a free-draining acid soil you can plant them directly in the garden. If not, buy some ericaceous (acid) compost, plant them in a container in a semi-shaded position and give them a high potash feed from time to time during the growing season. Use rainwater to water them rather than tap water, which contains lime, though if rainwater is scarce it is better to give them tap water than to allow them to dry out. Planting more than one variety will allow them to cross-pollinate and produce a higher yield. Once they are three years old, prune them between November and March, removing one or two of the oldest canes each year, along with any dead or diseased wood. The fruit is borne on shoots produced the previous year.

Blueberries on an individual bush ripen at different times, so you will need to gather them over a period. They will come away easily in your hand when they are ripe; start testing them a few days after they turn deep blue. According to variety, they ripen from early August to autumn. Store them in the refrigerator or freeze them for later use.

Cranberries

Cranberries are another 'superfood', containing plenty of antioxidants, vitamins and minerals. Most famously, though, they are a preventative against urinary infections, and it has recently been discovered that they may also act against the genital herpes virus. In the wild, they grow in peat bogs but they too will grow in containers with moist acid soils – wetter than blueberries require, but not saturated. They are low, trailing shrubs so are also suitable for hanging baskets.

Cranberries are self-pollinating, so you will not need to plant two varieties. Cut back any rambling stems in early spring, before growth begins.

The berries ripen in autumn and, because they contain a large

Eat blueberries to put you in the pink – they are a great source of antioxidants. With cream, they provide a delicious alternative to the more traditional strawberries and raspberries of summer days

amount of the natural preservative benzoic acid, will keep for months if stored in a cool place.

Nuts

Nuts are high in protein, fibre and essential amino acids, and walnuts are a good source of potassium and magnesium. English walnuts are considered the best for flavour, but the older varieties can be slow to produce a crop. Newer varieties such as 'Buccaneer' and 'Broadview' will crop within three or four years, and as these are compact they will do well in a container. You might also like to try an unusual variety called 'Red Danube', which has a red kernel. They will grow in many soils as long as they are moist but free-draining, and they need sunshine for the nuts to ripen properly. Keep young walnuts well watered, especially in their first spring before the buds break. See page 90 for decorative uses for them, too.

Hazelnuts are high in potassium, calcium, magnesium and vitamins, and in the form of cobnuts and filberts are a grand old tradition on the English table. In 1913, the national acreage of cobnut orchards, known as 'plats', was assessed at 2,964 hectares (7,325 acres), mainly in Kent. Now only 81–121 hectares (200–300 acres) remain, largely in the form of small orchards with trees a century old. However, the good news is that interest in cobnuts is reviving and new plats are being planted, with the Kentish Cobnuts Association (see page 94) promoting their cultivation and marketing.

Cobnuts are largely self-sterile, so you will need to plant at least two varieties to ensure they reproduce. 'Kentish Cob' is hardy and reliable, and can be pollinated by either 'Gunslebert', 'Merveille de Bollwiller' or 'Cosford', a variety with a particularly good flavour. They will grow in most types of soil, provided they are not waterlogged, but prefer a limy one. Store the harvested nuts in the refrigerator in an open container, with a little salt to help preserve them, and they will last until Christmas.

Start container-grown nuts in a 30cm (12in) diameter pot and move them to their final home in a 60cm (24in) container. Keep them well watered (but with well-drained soil) and prune dead or diseased stems in winter.

September

This month is characterized by warm days ebbing to cooler, damper weather. With the first morning mists of autumn, fruits ripening in the hedgerows and squirrels busy collecting nuts, the feel in the countryside is one of stocking up on nature's harvest before the pickings become slim.

September

SEPTEMBER IS OFTEN blessed with a period of warm and sunny weather, made all the sweeter for the knowledge that it is the last chance to enjoy the pleasure of strolling bare-armed with a gentle breeze caressing your skin. At any moment, you'll be reaching for a thick sweater, so no hot day should be taken for granted.

One of the most telling signs of autumn is the sight of swallows clustering on telegraph wires, getting ready for their migration to Africa. Meanwhile, wild swans and geese are arriving from their breeding sites in the Arctic to benefit from our milder winters and more plentiful supply of food. Resident birds are plundering hedgerows for berries, and wasps are gorging themselves on windfall fruits rotting in the grass. You too can feast on wild food this month, as long as you get there before the birds do. Try making jelly from rowanberries (*Sorbus aucuparia*) and from rose hips of our native dog rose (*Rosa canina*); and make wine, syrups, jellies and pies from elderberries.

As the month progresses and the weather becomes cooler and damper, wild fungi start to appear in meadows and woodlands. Seek them out to study their fascinating forms and beautiful colours, such as the blue shaggy inkcap and the white-spotted scarlet fly agaric, the toadstool on which pixies are invariably depicted. Harking back to our childhood memories as it does, this is a particularly endearing fungus; but it is highly poisonous, so leave it well alone.

The autumn collection of wild fungi has long been a favourite rite in some countries, for example Poland, and with the growing popularity of wild mushrooms in gourmet dishes the British fungi-hunter is no longer a rather solitary figure. Wild fungi are increasingly depleted in the countryside as they are now prolifically gathered for commercial purposes, so it's best to study them in situ, admire them and leave them alone. However, if you do wish to gather them to put on the table, make very sure you know what you are doing. There are many books on fungi with clear illustrations or, better still, go on a guided walk where you can learn about them – your local wildlife trust (see page 95) is a good place to enquire about these.

At the end of the month,

GROWING YOUR OWN MUSHROOMS

These days it's easy to grow your own mushrooms of various types and, with the increasing popularity of edible wild mushrooms, species such as black morels are becoming available to supplement the standard oysters and shiitake. You may prefer to buy complete kits such as a growbox with mushroom compost pre-sown with spawn, or a log that is ready to fruit. The latter will add to the natural appearance of your garden, particularly if you go for several of them, and they will also provide a habitat for various insects. Alternatively, you can introduce spawn to your own logs (oak is best, while coniferous wood is not suitable at all). Just drill holes in the wood, insert the spawn (also known as spores) and plug the holes with wax. Soak the log and leave it in a cool, damp place. However, you will probably have to wait a year for the mushrooms to emerge as opposed to two to three weeks for a previously impregnated log.

If you like the idea of edible mushrooms popping up in your lawn, bury pieces of manure impregnated with spawn about 5cm (2in) deep, preferably in a shady spot. You will need to keep the soil moist for success, but with a shady spot in an English autumn that is not difficult to do!

Michaelmas is one of the Quarter Days on which the country calendars turned. Rents were paid and hirings were begun and ended at fairs where employers negotiated with potential workers. These fairs were major festivals, with much feasting and drinking, and goose on the table for those who could afford it. Indeed, the gift of a goose often formed part of a tenancy agreement. In the days when people were literally sewn into their vests to provide some insulation all through the winter, Michaelmas must have been a last chance to let your hair down without shivering.

Hops have been used for their sleep-inducing qualities down the centuries

Making a hop pillow

Hops are renowned for their somniferous effects, so it's not surprising that they are often used in pillows to help induce a good night's sleep. Growing the hop vine (*Humulus lupulus* 'Aureus') will provide you with your own hops to dry, as well as beautiful bright yellow-green leaves to enhance your summer garden, but you can also buy hops without difficulty as they are used for home brewing.

Your pillow can be as easy or as complicated as you like, depending upon your skill and will with a needle. The most utilitarian way to create one is just to sew a muslin bag to contain the hops and slip it inside your pillowcase. However, it's not hard to machine sew three sides of a rectangle of pretty fabric to contain the muslin bag, handsewing the final seam shut once it is inserted. Incorporating some lace or broderie anglaise in the seams will add to the decorative effect. If you really enjoy needlework, use plain fabric and then embroider the pillow with motifs such as hop flowers and 'SLEEP WELL'. When the fragrance begins to fade, you can simply unpick the handsewn seam, take out the muslin bag and put a fresh supply of hops inside.

Your pillow will be more deliciously fragrant if you add herbs, spices and other aromatic goodies to the mix: allspice, dried orange peel, lemon balm, chamomile, lavender, lemon verbena, thyme or sweet marjoram.

Wrapping up the summer

THIS IS THE TIME OF YEAR when you'll be reaping the harvest of your labour in the kitchen garden, with carrots, beans, peas, courgettes, tomatoes, potatoes and onions all ripe for the picking. Most striking are giant pumpkins lying like great golden globes among their foliage, along with other squash such as 'Butternut' and the spectacular 'Turk's Turban'. For Hallowe'en purposes, leave the pumpkins in place until the foliage deteriorates (keeping the squash off the soil if it is a particularly wet year); otherwise, the way to judge whether a squash has reached full ripeness is by its colour. Harvest squash on a dry day and leave them balanced on bricks in the sun for a few days to 'set' the skin before storing in a frost-free shed.

Apples are ripening now. Early apples won't keep and should be eaten immediately, but later varieties will keep into the winter if they are stored correctly. Don't store any that have fallen from the tree or are otherwise blemished or wrinkled. Wrapping them in greaseproof paper will help to retain their moisture, but if you feel this is too much of a bother just put them straight onto a slatted surface so that air can circulate. Vegetable crates are obviously suitable, but you can also resort to freezer baskets or anything similar that comes to hand. Place them in a cool dark spot if possible.

Store potatoes in paper sacks, loosely tied at the top; put swedes,

A cattle show at The Royal Bath & West Show. Agricultural shows serve to promote the profile of agriculture, while providing a wonderful day out for all ages

carrots and parsnips in boxes, kept separate in beds of sand. Hang cabbages upside down, and when skins of garlic and onions are papery, plait them together by their foliage and hang them, too. Being able to eat your own vegetables way into winter will give you a great feeling of self-sufficiency, and there's nothing more delicious than coming home from a cold walk to a hearty home-grown vegetable soup simmering gently on the stove.

Sowing Afresh

As one crop is pulled from the ground, it's not too late to start another. Until the end of September, make fortnightly sowing of fast-growing salad crops such as rocket, 'Little Gem' lettuces and oriental greens including mustards and mibuna. You will have fresh leaves into the winter, though you might need to provide some protection with cloches as the weather hardens. In the areas of the UK with the hottest and driest summers, spinach will do better sown now, and it will grow all winter provided the season is a mild one. Make two or three sowings, again at fortnightly intervals, to give a steady supply for the table.

The best garlic comes from cloves planted in September, so take a few moments now to put some in and you'll have a stupendous supply of fresh garlic the following June or July. Plant the cloves about 15–18cm (6–7in) apart, with their tips just beneath the surface of the soil.

They will survive frost and snow but not waterlogged soil, so if yours is not well-drained make a raised bed for them. Make sure to rotate this crop to prevent disease, allowing at least three years to pass before planting in the same spot.

Country shows

September sees the last, and many of the biggest, country shows, and if you have put thought and effort into growing fruit and vegetables and caring for livestock, you'll find it fun to join in. You're bound to hear about local shows from other contestants who will be planning their bid to win prizes; if you wish to range further afield, the Association of Show and Agricultural Organisations (see page 94) lists nearly 400 shows throughout the UK and Eire.

To avoid causing annoyance to more established contestants, find out about dress codes and make sure that any livestock you enter have been trained to behave as well as possible. Even in the more jokey competitions such as the dog and owner that most resemble each other, it won't go down well if your dog causes an uproar.

If you have any ambition to beat experienced entrants with the size and glossiness of your garden produce, you will need to have this in mind long before the show date: competition starts at sowing time. But even if you've thought about it a little too late, entering in the knowledge that you don't stand a chance of a certificate will still be enjoyable and will give you good practice in presentation for the following year.

Specialist produce shows are great fun, where the profusion of a certain type of vegetable can make you think you must be dreaming: for example, the Totally Tomato Show at West Dean College in West Sussex, where more than 150 varieties of tomato are on display, or the Newent Onion Fayre on the Welsh borders. Here there are twenty-three classes covering all the edible members of the allium family, such as chives and leeks as well as shallots and onions, and competition is fierce. It is attended by about 15,000 people, and there's an onion-eating competition, folk bands, street entertainers and all kinds of jollity – but it has a serious purpose too, with six tonnes of onions sold on the day. Check out the website at www.newentonionfayre.co.uk and rejoice that there's still a thriving trade in produce that doesn't involve plastic wrapping and the supermarket shelf.

A Waddle and a Quack

GEESE ARE NATURE'S burglar alarm, and will provide you with eggs and fertilizer for your soil; as they are herbivores they will mow your lawn for you too, and act as intelligent and responsive pets. If you feel you haven't the space for geese, ducks are smaller and easier to handle. Either will give you a tasty alternative to hen's eggs and a good deal of amusement in watching their waddling forms and idiosyncratic ways.

Keeping geese

There are more than a dozen breeds of domestic geese in the UK, some descended from the European greylag goose and others from the wild Chinese swan goose. There are also crosses between the two. They are divided into heavy geese, medium geese and light geese, and as the heavy ones can weigh 15.5kg (34lb) you might like to try your hand first with one of the light breeds if you are a novice goose owner. The white Roman goose weighs only 4.5–6.3kg (10–14lb), and although it is not particularly interesting in appearance compared to some of the more ornamental breeds, it has an honourable history as being the type of goose that is said to have raised the alarm when the Gauls attacked Rome in the summer of 387 BC. They should give you up to sixty eggs a year, the surplus of which can be given away to friends and neighbours.

For something more graceful, Chinese geese are a little smaller, with long necks. They are the noisiest breed, and can be aggressive: make sure you buy hand-reared ones, which should be pleasant-tempered. Some strains lay eighty eggs a year. Sebastopols lay only half that number but the frizzle variety is decorative, with curly white or buff feathers. If you are more interested in temperament and appearance than the egg tally, Steinbachers are ideal. Introduced to the UK from Germany in the 1990s, they are grey or blue and possess a calm and friendly nature.

However, if you want to go for broke right from the start, with maximum size and striking appearance, African geese have a body 91cm (3ft) tall and a large imposing head, while the Toulouse have soft grey feathers, attractively patterned. Both make excellent pets.

You will need to provide your geese with a dry, solid home, ideally with a fox-proof run so that you can leave them with access to the outdoors in safety, if you will not be at home to marshal them indoors at dusk. A house measuring 2.4 x 1.8m (8 x 6ft) will be large enough for six average geese. Partitioning it off will give them individual nesting places. Straw is the ideal bedding for them, changed regularly.

Given a morning feed of wheat in the summer and layer pellets in the winter, geese will not require any further feeding in the day as long as they have adequate grazing. In dry, frosty or snowy weather you will need to give them an evening meal as well. There is no need to worry about when this might be necessary; a hungry goose is generally not slow to vocalize its complaint. A large garden will supply sufficient grazing for two or three geese; a 0.4 hectare (1 acre) patch of good grass will support ten to fifteen heavy geese or twenty light or medium ones.

Geese need constant access to water of a depth sufficient for them to immerse their heads while bathing. Though they will best enjoy a pond or running water, they can make do with old sinks or tubs, plunged into the ground. Sloping banks will be necessary for ponds and streams, and in the case of sinks, stepped bricks will give them a pathway in and out.

Keeping ducks

Ducks are also categorized as heavy and light, with further variations in the form of call ducks, Indian runners and bantam ducks. Heavy breeds tend to be those for the table, and as pets and egg layers you are more likely to want the light breeds such as the Khaki Campbell or the beautifully marked Abacot Ranger.

Call ducks and bantam ducks are hugely popular as pets, the latter having been placed in a separate,

Full of character and wonderful to look at, geese make very good 'guard dogs' too

miniature category after the growing number of call duck varieties was becoming unwieldy. They were once used to call down wild mallard to hunters' traps in the Fens and in Dutch marshes, and were known as decoy ducks, from the Dutch *de kooi*, meaning 'the trap' or 'cage'. It is thought they may have been imported from the Far East in the 1800s. Since the 1970s they have become hugely popular as exhibition birds, so you will find yourself bemused by the the choice of decorative varieties there are available to you. The Call Duck Association UK (see page 94) will be happy to fill you in on everything you need to know, from basic welfare to line breeding with an eye to winning trophies.

Indian runners are very unusual in appearance, standing tall and upright with long necks, and a head and beak at an angle not unlike the crook of a walking stick. As their name suggests, they run rather than waddle. Because of their vigour and profuse egg-laying, they were cross-bred with traditional table breeds to such an extent that the true Indian runner was nearly extinct in Britain at the beginning of the twentieth century. However, new stock was imported in the early 1900s to preserve the breed in this country and in 2000 the Indian Runner Duck Association (see page 94) was set up to look after the breed's welfare.

As with geese, ducks require a fox-proof house with a door at least 60cm (2ft) wide to avoid a jam as they rush to get out in the morning. Allow a minimum of 0.18sq m (2sq ft) per duck. Woodshavings topped with straw makes good bedding that can be added to in handfuls every few days and changed altogether once a month. The ducks will need clean straw on which to lay their eggs, which the majority of them do on ground level.

Ducks forage for food such as slugs, worms and greenstuff, but supplement this with morning and afternoon feeds: layer pellets and grain respectively. Like geese, they will need a source of water, and a daily bath is especially important in winter to keep their feathers in good condition to ward off the cold.

October

It's time for Britain to adopt its mantle of autumn colour, a final bounteous display before the year slips into the dormant season and brilliant colour becomes a rare sight in the countryside. The fields are ploughed and bare, and birds, squirrels and other wildlife are making the most of the wild harvest before winter sets in.

October

OCTOBER IS THE month for glorious autumn foliage, often set against pale blue skies and lit up by bright sunshine. It's a fabulous time for woodland walks, scuffling through fallen leaves. Beneath the horse chestnuts lie conkers, and if you are lucky enough to have sweet chestnut trees growing near your home, you can gather your own chestnuts to take home and roast on the fire.

This is the season when red deer are rutting, and you may hear the stags bellowing or even the clash of antlers as they fight rivals who are threatening to take over their hinds. While red deer normally flee at the approach of a human, during the rutting season stags are aggressive and dangerous, so don't approach for a closer look as you may be the next contestant they decide to fight.

Another characteristic sound of autumn is the melancholy honking of geese, which are now arriving in vast numbers from northern Europe and Russia to spend the winter feeding in British estuaries, along with swans and ducks which have made a similar journey. Fieldfares and redwings – winter thrushes – are beginning to arrive from the north, too, and you will mainly see them in ploughed fields, feeding in flocks. They will often be joined by skylarks, both resident birds and visitors from mainland Europe.

The hedgerows are beautiful at this time of year. Early morning dew bedecks cobwebs, and a few wildflowers are still in bloom. Red fruit such as rowanberries, haws and rosehips glow from among russeting leaves, offering a fine food source for blackbirds and others. Also to be seen now is the blue bloom of ripe sloes, the fruit of the blackthorn bush, *Prunus spinosa*, from which the famous sloe gin is derived. Sloe gin is usually made at Hallowe'en for drinking at Christmas, and the traditional advice is to gather sloes after the first frosts, as the cold removes some of their bitterness; however, a few hours in the freezer will suffice now that frosts tend to come later in the year. Wear very stout gloves, preferably of thick leather, when picking them,

PUMPKIN SOUP

Serves 4

This soup will keep for two days in the refrigerator and for two months in the freezer.

- 500g (1lb) pumpkin
- 25g (1oz) butter
- 1 medium onion, finely chopped
- 2 garlic cloves, crushed
- 750ml (1 1/4 pt) chicken stock
- 1/4 tsp grated nutmeg
- salt and pepper to taste
- 1 tablespoon freshly grated parmesan cheese, to serve

Chop the pumpkin into large cubes, discarding the rind and seeds. Melt the butter in a large saucepan and sweat the onion and garlic until the onion is translucent. Add the pumpkin and sweat for 2 minutes. Add the chicken stock, nutmeg and salt and pepper to taste, then cover and simmer for 20 minutes or until the pumpkin is tender. Blend the soup in a liquidizer or food processor. Serve sprinkled with grated Parmesan cheese.

Rosehips can be used to make rose hip jelly - but be sure to get there before the blackbirds

Sloe Gin

The longer the sloes are left to steep the better the gin will be. It will keep for up to three years.

- 450g (1lb) sloes
- 750ml (1 1/4 pt) gin
- 225g (8oz) sugar, or to taste

Wash and dry the sloes and prick them all over with a needle or skewer to pierce the skin. Put them into a large jar such as a Kilner jar that you will be able to seal tightly.

Cover the sloes with gin and add the sugar. Some people recommend 50g (2oz) per 600ml (1pt), so if you don't have a sweet tooth, use less than 225g (8oz). You can always add more to taste, but you can't take it away!

Seal the jar and leave for two to three months. Shake it every two to three days in the first month to dissolve the sugar, then once a week. When you are ready to drink it, strain it into clean bottles.

for a stab from a thorn on this bush can be very unpleasant indeed. It's not advisable to collect them from roadside hedges as they will be polluted.

Autumn is the time when hedgelaying is carried out. The current form of hedgelaying dates from the 1700s, and is done with the purpose of filling in the gaps between the plants' stems so that animals cannot push between them. Unwanted shoots are removed, then the stems are cut partly through and bent over to a diagonal angle. The lip remaining on the lower part of each stem is trimmed back, then stakes are driven in to hold the stems, or pleachers, in place.

Even if you don't need to keep animals enclosed, a layered hedge looks thick and healthy. As with many of the historic crafts, it is possible to go on training courses; contact the the National Hedgelaying Society (see pqge 94) for details. Hedgelaying styles vary from county to county, often geared to the type of stock the hedges were intended to enclose: the Midland or Bullock style, for example, comes from traditional beef-rearing areas, where hedges needed to be strong enough to resist bullocks, while the Westmorland style is designed for sheep.

October finishes of course with Hallowe'en and the carving of enormous pumpkin lanterns, their brilliant colour seeming to warm the whole house. Hallowe'en has its origins in ancient Celtic culture, when 31 October, known as Samhain, was celebrated as a feast for the dead. It was thought that the veil between the living and the dead was at its thinnest at this time of year, and places were set at the table for the deceased of earlier generations. The candles of the lanterns were intended to light the way for spirits, and apple-bobbing was linked to fortune-telling. The name Hallowe'en is a corruption of All Hallows' Eve; as often happened, the Church could not bring an end to the pagan custom so replaced it with a Christian festival, making 1 November a celebration of the saints – All Saints' Day.

Making Paper For Presents

NOW THAT TASKS in the garden are becoming a little mundane and there are days when the weather makes you disinclined to go out, you'll want to find a way of expressing your creative energies indoors, and perhaps get ahead with some homemade Christmas presents too.

The craft of making paper has a long and honourable history, from its beginnings in China in the first century AD. Early paper was formed from macerated vegetable fibre and tree bark, with the use of bamboo and rice straw developing over the next five centuries. Although the Chinese tried hard to keep the details of its manufacture secret, the process of papermaking spread eastwards throughout the Arabic world; it is believed that the first papermill may have been in Baghdad. It took 500 years, though, to arrive in Europe, by which time the paper tended to be made from hemp and flax. The first mention of cotton rag paper – the top-quality paper used by artists today – appears in a tract written by Peter, Abbot of Cluny, in the twelfth century, and by the thirteenth century Fabriano in Italy had become a centre for the papermaking industry, with numerous papermills driven by water power. The term 'foolscap' to describe a size of paper is not, as commonly thought, due to being the perfect size for making a dunce's cap, but rather harks back to the days when paper was watermarked with emblems understandable to those who could not read measurements; one of the emblems was a jester's cap.

Clearly, papermaking can be a highly skilled task, but it's not hard to make paper in a simple fashion at home, with minimal equipment. If you are one of those many people who can't resist well-stocked stationery shops with pretty papers on show, you'll revel in doing it yourself.

Equipment

Other than some fairly basic kitchen equipment, you will need a mould. This is a wooden frame with a mesh stretched across it to act as a sieve. You can make a frame very easily by glueing or nailing four pieces of wood together; use 20 x 50mm ($^3/_4$ x 2in) wood, and make the inner length and width the size of the paper you wish to make. The 20mm ($^3/_4$ in) measurement is the surface width, with 50mm (2in) being the depth of the frame. If you're not good at this sort of thing, ask your local picture framer to knock it up for you from inexpensive moulding. Cover this frame with tightly stretched mesh – for example, mosquito mesh or just a piece of net curtain – nailed to the edge of the frame.

You will also need a large container: a baby bath will suffice, or, if you are starting small, a washing-up bowl.

Making the pulp

Collect together a variety of unwanted paper. Avoid newspaper (which will discolour) and glossy magazines, but tissues and kitchen towels, any art paper, envelopes, copier paper and so forth are all suitable.

Tear the paper into pieces about 25mm (1in) in size and soak it in water. How long for depends on the quality of paper; tissues will be ready in less than an hour, while cotton rag watercolour paper may take up to three days. Using boiling water will speed up the process considerably.

Next, macerate the paper in a blender or food processor, adding 550ml (16fl oz) of water to each small handful of paper. You need to blend only until the fibres separate, so start at very short times of about fifteen seconds and pause to examine the result. If there are still large pieces of paper intact, give it another go. You don't want it to be

absolutely smooth, though, as you will lose some of the attractive handmade quality.

Pour the pulp into your container. A blenderful will make one thin A4 sheet, so carry on until you have made as much as you think you will need.

MAKING THE PAPER

Now, to make paper with a truly country feel, add some feathers or pressed ferns, leaves or flowers; if you are planning a Christmas present for a friend who is particularly fond of some of your plants, incorporating them into a gift of paper is a most individual way of evoking memories of your garden. If you would like to colour the paper too, the choice is wide: blueberry or beetroot juice, onion skins, turmeric, tea and coffee will give natural colours, or you can buy dyes such as Dylon from chemists, craft shops and department stores. Simply stir into the pulp until you have the sort of colour you want, remembering that it will become lighter as it dries.

Give the pulp a good stir. Dip the frame vertically into the far side of the container, then, in one smooth movement, tilt it towards you so that it is lying horizontally beneath the pulp and lift it out, holding it level. Quickly, before the water has drained off, give it a little shake. If you are slow about doing this the paper will tear because there is not enough water left.

Leave the frame on some newspaper until the pulp has fully drained, then place it outdoors in a sheltered spot in the sun, tilted upright. If the weather is poor, a position next to a heater indoors will do instead. Depending on the consistency of the paper and the drying conditions, it will take anything from two to twenty-four hours to dry. Finally, peel it from the mould using a palette knife.

You can now use your paper as a whole sheet, or fold it to make cards. The easiest way to make matching envelopes is to steam the glue from an ordinary envelope of the appropriate size and use it as a template to cut your own paper to shape.

Handmade paper has a lovely homemade texture to it, and is a wonderful craft to pursue in these days of email and texting

November

November is a month when autumn moves inexorably into winter, but as chilly weather sets in there is plenty to look forward to on country walks, and the pleasure of log fires in the grate and hearty casseroles simmering on the stove.

November

AT THE BEGINNING of the month there are still green leaves among the red, russet and yellow of the trees, but this is November and by its end sharp winds will have ripped most of the foliage from the branches, leaving them stark and bare. As the year progresses to its final month, the colour in the countryside is dying too, with bright colours giving way to sombre greys and browns, punctuated by the brilliant white of frost on clear days.

Yet the more subtle tones have their beauty too, and such vivid colour as there is makes its presence felt all the more: along the dark hedges are the scarlet and crimson of bryony, guelder rose and hawthorn berries.

On the forest floor where oaks and beeches grow you may find clusters of deep yellow chanterelle mushrooms, delicious fried in a little butter. Some species of bracket fungi, for example *Fistulina hepatica* (beefsteak fungus, or ox-tongue, named after its meaty flesh and the blood-red liquid it oozes when cut), are edible but, as ever, treat wild fungi with great caution and do not attempt experimentation. Many of these species live in symbiotic relationship with trees, absorbing water and minerals for them and in turn benefiting from their nutrients. The beefsteak fungus feeds off the heartwood of oak trees, turning it redder in colour, which makes it very attractive to furniture makers.

The forest floor also provides sustenance for many others than a passing human with a taste for fungi: beechnuts, acorns, hazelnuts and pine cones provide food for woodland mammals and birds, with magpies, jays and squirrels all competing for nuts.

STEAK AND KIDNEY PUDDING
Serves 6

Hearty meat puddings and pies are a traditional favourite to provide warming food against the British winter, and they are coming back into fashion. Steak and kidney pudding is a long-standing staple, which often had the added luxury of oysters in Victorian times.

For the suet crust pastry:
- 300g (10oz) white self-raising flour
- 150g (5oz) shredded suet
- salt and pepper
- butter, for greasing

For the filling:
- 4 tbsp vegetable oil
- 700g (1 1/2lb) chuck steak, cubed
- 225g (8oz) ox kidney, cubed
- 1 medium onion, sliced
- 2 tbsp white plain flour
- 600ml (1pt) beef stock
- dash of Worcestershire sauce
- 2 tbsp chopped fresh parsley

Preheat the oven to 170°C/325°F/Gas Mark 3. Heat the oil in a flameproof casserole, then add the steak and kidney in batches, browning them and removing them to drain on some kitchen towel. Add the onion to the pan and cook until lightly brown.

Off the heat, stir in the flour and stock and add the Worcestershire sauce and seasoning to taste. Bring to the boil and return the steak and kidney to the casserole. Cover and cook in the oven for about 2 hours or until the meat is tender. Check the seasoning, stir in the parsley and set aside.

To make the suet crust pastry, mix the flour, suet and seasoning together and add enough water to bind it to a soft dough, about 175–200ml, (6–7fl oz). Knead until smooth. Cut off one quarter and roll out the rest to line a well-buttered 1.7 litre (3pt) pudding basin, overlapping the join.

Spoon in the contents of the casserole, then roll out the remaining quarter of the dough and use it to make a lid, damping the edges to form a seal with the lining. Cover the basin with a double sheet of foil, pleated in the centre to allow room for expansion. Tie it securely with string and place it in a steamer over boiling water, or, if you don't have a steamer, on a saucer in a covered pan of boiling water. Boil for 2 hours, replenishing the water when necessary.

This is a great time of year for birdwatching, with diminishing foliage making them much easier to see. Siskins, which spend the summer in Scottish conifer forests, travel in flocks and are a charming sight; although they are finches, their nimble style of extracting food from catkins and cones is more akin to that of tits. Another type of visiting finch is the brambling, which you will find feeding on beechnuts. You may spot bullfinches tucking into the dried remains of blackberries, and if you see blackbirds in a flock, these will be visitors from Scandinavia which are much more sociable than our native blackbird. Along the coast and on inland waterways and marshes you will see whooper swans from Iceland, Bewick's swans from Siberia and ducks such as wigeon, shovellers and teal, while pink-footed geese head inland for stubble fields during the day.

If you haven't already got nesting boxes in the garden, now is the time to put them up as they will provide a roost for birds over winter and also become part of the scenery, ready for nesting in spring. Stock up your bird table regularly (see page 12), and many of the birds which come to you for food when the natural supply is running low will continue to visit your garden in the summer too. If you also have berried plants such as cotoneaster, pyracantha, berberis and holly you will be providing a valuable service. Many birds such as tits and finches love clematis seeds, both from garden plants and from wild *Clematis vitalba*, which is adorning hedgerows with its silvery, feathery seedheads.

Where once it was considered desirable to tidy the garden as much as possible for winter, this is the last thing to do if you want to encourage wildlife. Leaf litter, old logs and decaying vegetation all provide a shelter for wildlife, and if you buy some hedgehog boxes you will be even surer to attract some prickly visitors who will reduce your slug population come the spring.

Our main celebration this month is of course Guy Fawkes Night which, although ostensibly commemorating the plot to blow up Parliament on 5 November 1605, probably dates from pagan traditions of bonfires and sacrifices; dummies were burned on bonfires in November from the mid-thirteenth century or even

Remember, remember. Sparklers are a great way to introduce young children to fireworks, as long as they are supervised

earlier, with the aim of driving away evil spirits as the old year came to an end. Although fireworks have become more and more elaborate in recent years, there's still enchantment in the humble sparkler, a roaring bonfire and a charred spud. But leave building the bonfire until the day itself, and check it carefully, to avoid harming any shelter-seeking hedgehogs who are inclined to see a waiting pile of logs and branches as a good sleeping place.

NATURAL WOOL DYEING

BECAUSE OF THE RELATIVE fragility of textiles it is not known where or when the practice of using natural dyes to colour them began. However, it definitely dates back more than 4,000 years, with written records from China dated 2,600 BC and fragments surviving from Minoan civilization. Colours such as madder (used in fabrics found in King Tutankhamen's tomb) and indigo were derived from plants and were easy to obtain; the purple used for royal robes in the time of Alexander the Great – and indeed the colour that is still associated with royalty – was restricted to elite society because it was derived from just one vein of a crustacean found near Tyre. It is estimated that about 8,500 shellfish were required to produce 1 gram of dye, making its value well beyond the reach of wider society.

Its long history makes the dyeing of textiles with natural colours a highly satisfying thing to do, continuing an unbroken line stretching down through human civilizations. It also produces soft, warm colours that are particularly well suited to wool, especially when it is knitted into traditional patterns where the slight variation in the colour will add to the homespun look.

Natural dyes fall into three categories: vegetable (such as indigo), animal (such as cochineal, from a beetle) and mineral (such as ochre). Many of the dyes can be obtained from your own garden or those of your neighbours, or gathered from the wild; others can be bought relatively inexpensively. Some are adjective dyes, meaning that they require a mordant to absorb and fix the colour; substantive dyes, which include lichens, oak galls and walnut husks, do not. The most common mordants are alum, iron, tin and tannic acid, and each will produce a different colour which will also vary, depending on the textile you are dyeing. Some mordants are toxic, so

DYE COLOURS WITH WOOL AND ALUM MORDANT

GARDEN PLANTS

- *Achillea millefolium* (Yarrow) flowers .... yellow
- *Alchemilla vulgaris* (Ladies' mantle) stems, leaves and flowers .... yellow
- *Allium cepa* (Onion) skins
  yellow skins .... orange/brown
  red skins .... red-brown/dark tan
- *Baptisia* (False indigo) leaves .... blue
- *Isatis tinctoria* (Woad) leaves .... blue
- *Sanguinaria canadensis* (Bloodroot) root .... orange
- *Stachys officinalis* (Betony) all parts .... green

FUNGI

- *Cortinarius sanguineus* (Bloodred webcap) .... red/red-orange
- *Fomes fomentarius* (Hoof fungus/Tinder bracket) .... beige/mustard
- *Gymnopilus penetrans* (Common rustgill) .... gold
- *Inonotus hispidus* (Shaggy bracket) .... yellow

you should wear an apron and gloves when using them. Needless to say, you would not in any case want to wear your best clothes when splashing dye about. Dyes, mordants and natural unbleached wool can all be obtained from craft suppliers.

The equipment you need is simple: a large stainless steel or enamel saucepan; kitchen scales; measuring spoons; a smooth stick or wooden spoon for stirring; and some muslin.

First divide the wool into skeins of manageable size (or weighed amounts if you are using different colours for a specific pattern) and tie them very loosely. Unless the wool is supplied ready-to-dye, you will need to wash it first in mild, neutral soap. The next step is to mordant it. Dissolve one tablespoon of alum and ½ tablespoon cream of tartar in a cup of warm water, then add to 4.5 litres (1 gallon) warm water. Soak the wool in warm water, then add to the mordant, bring it up to simmering point and simmer for about one hour. Remove the wool from the mordant and rinse it. You can then dry it in a warm, dark place and keep it in the refrigerator for up to three weeks, or proceed to dye it immediately.

Most natural dyestuffs are put into sufficient cold water to cover them and heated up slowly. Break your materials into small pieces – onion skins, for example, won't dissolve – before adding them to the water. The amount of material that you will need will depend upon the depth of colour you want: a good start for experimentation with much plant material is 100g (4oz) per 450g (1lb) wool, but if you like exact instructions before you start, you will be able to find plenty of recipes for various dyes on the internet and in books (see pages 94–95). Simmer the plant material for about one hour, or until most of the colour has leached out, then strain through muslin.

Naturally dyed wool will not be so vibrantly coloured as synthetically dyed wool, but it is still attractive, and kinder to the environment

Next, warm 4.5 litres (1 gallon) water in a clean pan, add the dyestuff and stir well. Add the wool, stir gently, bring to the boil and then simmer until the wool has reached the desired colour. Bear in mind it will lighten when it is washed and dried, so at this stage it should be darker than you want. Each subsequent batch of wool in the same dye solution will require approximately twice as long to reach the same colour as the dye becomes exhausted.

Rinse the wool on removing from the dyebath, using water of the same temperature, and then cooling it progressively as you continue to rinse until the water is clear. Gently squeeze the wool dry or blot it with a towel, then hang on a washing line until it is dry.

December

With December comes the end of the year, the shortest day and sometimes forbidding weather. But with Christmas festivities, the house is alight with warmth and festooned with pretty decorations, the fragrance of pine branches pervades the air and presents are wrapped temptingly in brightly coloured paper.

December

THIS TIME OF YEAR was once largely bereft of flowers other than autumn crocus and the Christmas rose, but with climate change it is becoming not unusual to see a cherry tree in bloom at Christmas. But still, garden interest is mainly concerned with architectural stems, outlined with frost on cold days and backlit by low sun – a fabulous sight that more than matches the glories of summer for visual appeal. You can add to it by planting the ornamental brambles *Rubus thibetanus* or *Rubus cockburnianus*, which have prickly shoots that take on a brilliant white bloom in winter, giving an impression of hoar frost even where none exists. For maximum architectural effect, plant them against a dark background such as a yew hedge or black-painted panel fence where their shoots will stand out all the more starkly.

If you have a garden pond it may often freeze in December and, pretty though that may look in low sun, remember that wildlife needs access to water and in particular birds need to bathe, no matter how cold it is. If you watch individual blackbirds carefully you may even discover that they have a particular time of day they like to take their bath, turning up promptly as if responding to an internal alarm clock. So take care to break the ice each day, and even several times a day when the temperature is low enough for it to constantly refreeze.

There are still plenty of red berries for the birds about, and some years you may see waxwings feeding upon them. Easily recognized by their pinkish body, black bib and yellow flash on wings and tail, they sometimes arrive in large numbers if the berry supply is low in Scandinavia; if there is plenty to eat at home, few may bother to make the flight.

Of course, at this time of year there are two berries of major interest to humans: holly and mistletoe. Birds don't care for the former much, so you will be robbing no one of their dinner by cutting branches off for the Christmas decorations. Mistletoe is more popular with birds and more difficult for you to access, as it usually grows quite high above the ground. You will recognize it by its ball-shaped bunches, not unlike birds' nests,

adorning the bare branches of deciduous trees which it has parasitized. The berries are very sticky, and it spreads to new sites by means of birds wiping their beaks on other branches. The practice of hanging it in the home is believed to go back to Druidic times, when it was thought to bring good luck and ward off evil spirits.

Christmas wouldn't be Christmas without holly and mistletoe, and also robins and wreaths. The real bird in the garden is at it boldest (and that means very bold) at this time of year when food is scarce, and you'll find it very tame indeed, at times even in your kitchen when the frost really bites and the ground is solid. While you are stocking up on Christmas food, remember to keep the bird

Gilded walnuts

Gilded walnuts were popular Christmas decorations in Victorian times, when they contained a motto or motif that told the fortunes of the person opening the nut. You can have fun making these too, to give as presents or use them as pretty decoration.

Crack open the nut, taking care not to damage either of the two halves. Extract the kernel and then put in the 'fortune'. For example, if you have young children with artistic talent or a great love of horses, you might put in a little image of a brush or a horse respectively. Older children may regard such low-tech efforts with withering scorn, while adults will probably be charmed by the thought of long-gone traditions – you will need to judge your audience here!

Glue the halves together, then, when the glue is dry, work a tin-tack into the hole where the stem once was. Gild the nut and tack with paint from a craft shop, then tie to the tree with gold metallic string.

Robins provide a lovely flash of colour around the garden at this time. Encourage them with bird feeders and a bird bath that is kept unfrozen

table well stocked too, as a bird needs to eat its own body weight each day to survive the cold night.

Even if you don't care to light one every day, you will probably want to have a roaring log fire over Christmas. The Yule log is an old tradition, and the charred remains of it were thought to guard the house against fire and lightning, while the ashes were scattered over surrounding fields to bring good harvests the following year. The celebration of Christmas is an amalgam of various pagan rituals relating to the winter solstice overlaid by Christian tradition, and we can enjoy the sense of history by drawing on both.

Making a Pomander

A fragrant pomander is a delightful and traditional Christmas decoration, and is easy to make.

Using a skewer or fork, pierce holes in an orange. You can do this in a neat pattern, randomly or densely; but in the latter case, make sure the holes don't run into each other. Push whole cloves into each hole, where they will fit snugly.

If you have covered the orange completely, you can now roll it in a mixture of cinnamon, allspice and nutmeg. Place the orange in the oven at a very low heat and bake for one hour to cure it. If you are using spices, roll the orange over once a day for a week and leave it to dry in a cool dark place. This type of pomander will last indefinitely.

Display the pomander in a pretty basket or suspend it from ribbons criss-crossed around it.

Découpage

DÉCOUPAGE IS ANOTHER of those traditional crafts that are coming back into fashion as we look for respite from the constant stream of new technological marvels taking over our world. The art of cutting out paper images and applying them to various objects and even walls, it first began in Italy and France in the eighteenth century and became highly popular in England in the nineteenth century, being thought a very suitable occupation for Victorian ladies. However, though the technique is traditional, the results can be updated to look as modern and funky as you like, simply by using images that suit the style.

The Victorians didn't have access to the wealth of coloured print material we have today, so black and white patterns were coloured with watercolours. With all the art materials that are available now, you have far greater potential for colour experimentation: with découpage you can restrict yourself to cutting out ready-made images or be as creative as you like.

You will need to prepare the base so that it is smooth. It's best to start with easy objects with flat surfaces that are already clean; a piece of inexpensive wooden furniture from a chain store will allow you to get to the fun bit faster than old furniture that may first need to have lumpy, ancient varnish stripped back. Bare new wood will require a coat of shellac to stop the sap seeping out, but that is very quick and easy to do by comparison. In the case of varnished new furniture you can apply the découpage directly to it, or paint it first with the desired colour.

When it comes to your choice of paper, wrapping paper, catalogues and magazines will give you numerous pictures and you can make colour photocopies of pictures in books that you don't wish to destroy. If you decide you

Sharp scissors, a steady hand and good light are a must for the delicate skill of découpage

want monochrome images, old books and catalogues are a good source. Alternatively, you can make black and white photocopies of coloured images. This works best with paintings, where the artist has thought about the tonal range in his or her work, rather than with photographs where colour is the main purpose, such as those designed to show what a product looks like.

Even with new furniture, you will probably have to do a little filling of holes or obtrusive grain. Sand first with fine sandpaper, then wipe with a damp sponge before applying the filler.

Applying your images

To cut out your images, you can use scissors or a craft knife, or indeed a scalpel for intricate detail. If the paper is thin or delicate, it is a good idea to seal it first with water-based varnish, which will take about ten minutes or more to dry. Take great care with the cutting stage, because awkward angles or extraneous white paper around an image will really show up.

The next step is to glue your images to your base. Use starch glue or white glue for preference; gum glue can give a brownish tinge. Apply it to the base, not the paper, and spread it with your finger as evenly as possible. Place your image in position and smooth it down, working from one side to another to expel any air bubbles and making sure that the edges are firmly pressed down. Then wipe across it with a damp sponge or cloth and dab off any excess glue around the edges; don't skimp on this as it will get dirty and the varnish may not adhere to it. If you are using large images you may prefer to smooth them down with a roller, in which case you should roll from the centre outwards, working quickly before any air bubbles form as these may press out into creases.

Varnishing

Découpage is finished with a varnish thick enough to leave a completely smooth surface so that the edges of the paper cannot be felt – you will need to apply about ten coats. Modern acrylic (water-based) varnishes dry quickly and are completely clear, though if you wish to you can tint them with pigment to add colour. This can be useful to unify colours where some are looking a little too bright to sit well with the rest.

Traditional varnishes, such as oil-based and shellac, give a slight yellow tinge that will give an antique effect. To take this even further you can buy crackle varnish which is laid over an oil-based one that is partially dry; the drier it is, the smaller the cracks will be. They will appear as the crackle varnish dries.

Making your design

The basic technique of découpage is easy; it just requires care and time. Placing motifs here and there, perhaps following a certain theme, is quite easy too. However, a complicated piece of traditional découpage, with overlapping cutouts, can seem daunting. The way to tackle it is to arrange your pieces first on a flat surface, shuffling them around until your design is to your liking. Then, following the same arrangement, fix them to your base with a little mounting putty or sticky tape. Fix tracing paper over the top with mounting putty and trace your design as a final marker of where your pieces of paper will go. Finally, peel back the tracing paper a little at a time and glue your paper bit by bit, replacing the tracing paper to check the positioning.

Christmas presents

Découpage is excellent for unusual Christmas presents with a personal feel. Consider decorating simple boxes, picture frames, letter racks and mirrors. You could even decorate the bottles of your homemade sloe gin (see page 79) to give an added flourish to your gift. You can also tackle bigger objects without it turning into a major job if you simply paint the greater part in solid colour and just decorate here and there – for example a child's chest of drawers where just the drawer fronts have motifs. If you are reasonably confident of your skills as an artist, handpainting a scene and adding motifs into it – figures placed into a landscape, for instance – gives a delightful effect.

Find Out More

Organizations

Association of Show and Agricultural Organisations
Tel: 01737 645857
www.asao.co.uk
Whether you wish to organize or attend a show, the ASAO will be able to offer information.

British Angora Goat Society
Tel: 01789 841931
www.britishangoragoats.org.uk
Provides information on keeping angora goats and organizes an annual show.

British Beekeepers Association
Tel: 02476 696679
www.bbka.org.uk
Offers events, courses and support boards on the website.

British Camelids Association
01608 661893
www.llama.co.uk
The Association organizes shows, social events, the breeders' directory, workshops and conferences and publishes a quarterly journal.

British Waterfowl Association
Tel: 01892 740212
www.waterfowl.org.uk
Join the BWA for information on both wild and domestic waterfowl.

Call Duck Association UK
Tel: 01558 650532
www.callducks.net
Information on call duck varieties, welfare and management.

English Folk Dance and Song Society
Tel: 020 7485 2206
www.efdss.org
Information on traditional song and dance, including lists of teachers.

HDRA
Tel: 02476 303517
www.hdra.org.uk
Europe's largest organic membership organization, dedicated to researching and promoting organic gardening, farming and food. Members gain access to advice, events and their Heritage Seed Library.

Herb Society
Tel: 01295 768899
www.herbsociety.co.uk
The Society aims to provide information of interest to growers, gardeners, botanists, historians, cooks, aromatherapists, beauticians and garden designers. Members get discounts at participating nurseries and suppliers.

Indian Runner Duck Association
Richard Sadler (Membership Secretary), 14 Birchin Lane, Nantwich, Cheshire, CW5 6JT
www.runnerduck.net
The Association provides information on the health, welfare and breeding of runner ducks.

Kentish Cobnuts Association
Tel: 01732 882734
www.kentishcobnutsassociation.co.uk
The website gives advice on growing cobnuts and lists suppliers of both trees and nuts.

National Hedgelaying Society
Tel: 01491 61350
www.hedgelaying.org.uk
The Society aims to encourage the art of hedgelaying and keep the local styles in existence.

National Vegetable Society
Tel: 01614 427190
www.nvsuk.org.uk
The NVS aims to help kitchen gardeners with the growing of their vegetables and offers members a chance to meet enthusiastic and knowledgeable growers, and to take part in their local annual shows.

Natural Dyes International
www.naturaldyes.org
A non-profit organization for research into natural dyes and pigments, based in the USA.

People's Trust for Endangered Species
Tel: 020 7498 4533
www.ptes.org
The People's Trust takes on a range of projects for endangered and threatened species and their habitats all over the world. It organizes wildlife-watching events led by wildlife experts around the UK.

Royal Horticultural Society
Tel: 020 7834 4333
www.rhs.org.uk
The UK's leading garden charity.

Royal Society for the Protection of Birds (RSPB)
Tel: 01767 680551
www.rspb.org.uk
The RSPB is a wildlife conservation charity with more than a million members. There are over 150 RSPB nature reserves to visit throughout the UK, covering more than 97 hectares (240,000 acres).